INGHAM   U

# THEORY OF MONEY

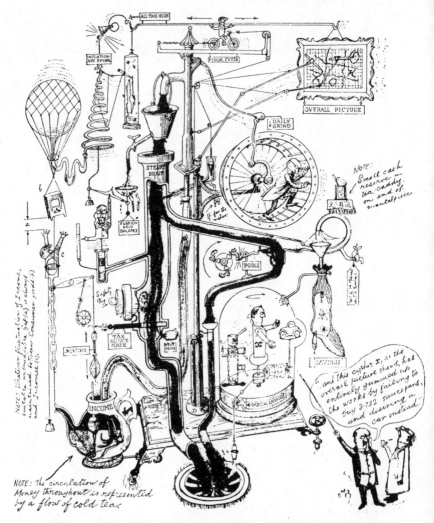

**MACHINE DESIGNED TO SHOW THE WORKING OF THE ECONOMIC SYSTEM**

Emett's delightful drawing, which is reproduced for the enjoyment of readers by kind permission of the proprietors of *Punch*, was inspired by a demonstration of the Phillips/Newlyn hydraulic machine built as a teaching device and upon which the flow diagram in this book is based.

# THEORY OF MONEY

BY

W. T. NEWLYN
AND
R. P. BOOTLE

THIRD EDITION

CLARENDON PRESS · OXFORD

1978

*Oxford University Press, Walton Street, Oxford,* OX2 6DP

OXFORD LONDON GLASGOW
NEW YORK TORONTO MELBOURNE WELLINGTON
KUALA LUMPUR SINGAPORE JAKARTA HONG KONG TOKYO
DELHI BOMBAY CALCUTTA MADRAS KARACHI
IBADAN NAIROBI DAR ES SALAAM CAPE TOWN

© *Oxford University Press 1962, 1971, 1978*

FIRST EDITION 1962
SECOND EDITION 1971
THIRD EDITION 1978

**British Library Cataloguing in Publication Data**

Newlyn, Walter Tessier
    Theory of money. — 3rd ed.
    1. Money
    I. Title   II. Bootle, R R
    332.4'01   HG221   78-40249

ISBN 0-19-877099-5
ISBN 0-19-877100-2 Pbk.

*Typeset by Eta Services (Typesetters) Ltd., Beccles, Suffolk and Printed in Great Britain by Richard Clay & Co. Ltd., Bungay, Suffolk*

# PREFACE

IN venturing on a third edition of this book I was conscious of three major considerations. Firstly that the revisions made in the second edition were unsatisfactory. Secondly that the subject had developed so much as a result of escalating interest by academics and policy makers that a radical revision was required. Thirdly that the extent of my involvement in another major area of economics put the task beyond my capacity unaided. I have been most fortunate in finding in Roger Bootle a collaborator who has borne the main burden of the revision, which we have been able to base on close agreement on fundamentals and presentation. It is appropriate therefore that the rest of this preface should reflect the joint authorship of the book.

W.T.N.

The principal function of a preface to a book which is intended as a text for use in higher education is that of explaining how it fits into the existing literature. We believe that *Theory of Money* has a distinct role in covering rigorously, but non-mathematically, the whole of the theory of monetary behaviour and policy. We see it as a bridge between the simple treatment in an undergraduate course in macro economics, and specialist study.

In our revision we have retained the basic structure of the book but have increased the generality of the theory by reference to different monetary systems, confining consideration of the United Kingdom system to the final chapter, which, as in previous editions, deals with application. Consistently with the desirability of starting by establishing basic principles, the first five chapters remain substantially unaltered except for some pruning and clarification. The rest has been largely rewritten and extended so as successively to remove simplifying assumptions and incorporate new theoretical developments. In particular we have attempted differentiation and integration of the 'Keynesian' and 'monetarist' approaches as appropriate.

Although there has been a great increase in empirical work

since the lack of it was noted in the second edition, it is still true to say that econometrics has not yet succeeded in giving convincing answers to the major empirical questions on which there is *a priori* disagreement among monetary economists. We hope that, at least, we have put these empirical differences into a theoretical context in which the greatly exaggerated opposition between 'Keynesians' and 'monetarists' is reduced to a minimum.

Finally we record our gratitude to Anthony S. Courakis (Brasenose College, Oxford) and John Brothwell (University of Leeds) for useful discussions on many issues dealt with in the book, but no responsibility for what we have written attaches to either.

R. P. BOOTLE
*St. Anne's College,*
*Oxford*

W. T. NEWLYN
*School of Economic Studies,*
*Leeds*

# CONTENTS

# LIST OF FIGURES

# LIST OF TABLES

# I

## WHAT IS MONEY?

THE essential function, which enables us to identify money, is that it is generally accepted as a means of payment. The necessity of having something to perform this exchange function lies in the fact that, in the absence of such a medium, exchange requires a double coincidence of wants. Thus, in a barter system, a seller of an article must not only find someone who is willing to give value for it but someone who is also willing to give in exchange some article which the seller wishes to acquire. Alternatively he must arrange a multilateral series of barter transactions having the same final result. The complications of such barter arrangements clearly restrict the opportunity for exchange so severely that little progress could have been made towards a complex exchange economy without the introduction of a common medium of exchange.

Once such a medium is introduced, the single transaction of barter becomes decomposed into separate transactions of sale and purchase, and the double coincidence is eliminated. But this separation into two transactions involves more than a simple separation of two elements which were previously implicit in the barter transaction; the introduction of money also necessarily separates the transactions in time. The only circumstances in which the interval between the sale of goods and the use of the money obtained for them could be zero would be circumstances in which the double coincidence of wants is present, either in a bilateral or a multilateral arrangement, and a medium of exchange would therefore be redundant. The general acceptability of anything as a medium of exchange thus necessarily implies that, to some extent, it will be held over time.

In a modern economy incomes consist of wages, salaries, interest, rent, and profits, which are payments for the services contributing to the manufacture and sale of goods. Such payments are received discontinuously and spent discontinuously, and the dating of expenditures does not coincide with that of income receipts. No one pays out the whole of his weekly or monthly income the moment it is received, though many of us may think this is very nearly true in our own case. Similarly the multitude of intermediate transactions which are involved in the production of goods involve intervals between payment and receipt. To a considerable extent therefore, money must necessarily act as a store of value by virtue of its use as a medium of exchange.

In fact, as will be shown in a later chapter, money is actually used as a store of value to a much greater extent than that which is necessarily involved in its exchange function. We shall distinguish this additional function of money as its asset function. For the purpose of analysis it will be necessary to treat these two functions separately, but it will subsequently be argued that they are not distinct. The asset function of money is of crucial importance in monetary theory, but the performance of this function is not necessary to a definition of money. A medium of exchange is money even though it serves as an asset to no greater extent than is necessarily implied in its exchange function.

Two other functions are generally performed by money, that of acting as a unit of account and that of acting as a standard of deferred payment. Neither of these is either a necessary or a sufficient condition. It is possible to have a unit of account which does not exist in any monetary form; the guinea is an example; generally, however, the unit of account will correspond with the monetary unit. Again, money, by virtue of acting as the medium of exchange, will generally be used as a standard for deferred payment, but this is not necessarily the case; the use of money as a standard of deferred payment is very closely related to its asset function, but such use is not a necessary characteristic of money. This does not mean that it is a matter of no importance whether or not money acts in this way; indeed this will be a major issue in the subsequent analysis.

We return then to our original definition: anything is money which functions generally as a medium of exchange. The necessary condition for the performance of this exchange function is general acceptability in settlement of debt. General acceptability may come about as a result of a number of different factors operating singly or in combination; it falls within that perplexing but fascinating group of phenomena which is affected by self-justifying beliefs. If the members of a community think that money will be generally acceptable, then it will be; otherwise not.

One of the factors which may contribute to establishing the acceptability of money is its legal status. Money may be made legal tender, that is to say, payment in that money will be deemed by the courts to be full satisfaction of debts. Money which has such a status is called *legal money* while money which has no such status is called *customary money*. This differentiation between legal and customary money is more the concern of the lawyer and historian than the economist; a much more significant distinction from the point of view of the economist is that between *commodity money* and *token money*. Commodity money is a medium of exchange which has a commodity value as distinct from the value which it has acquired by being generally acceptable in exchange for goods and services. Its commodity value is that which it would have if it were not used as money. Token money on the other hand has, in the limiting case of paper notes, no commodity value whatever; its value derives entirely from the fact that it is generally acceptable in exchange for goods and services.

Indeed token money need not take a physical form at all. The vast majority of payments (by value) in a modern economy is made by means of entries in bank ledgers and these are increasingly being effected by computers. Here the payment is made not by the transfer of some physical entity but by the alteration of a financial relationship. A bank customer making a payment instructs his bank, by writing a cheque, to transfer part of his claim on the bank (his deposit) to the payee. Since such transfers of bank deposits are generally accepted in settlement of a debt we must include bank deposits in the category of money in accordance with our functional definition.

In order to see that this statement is correct it is essential that we should have regard to the deposit, not to the instrument which transfers the deposit. A cheque is not money; it is simply a written order to transfer money; only the deposit itself is money. Thus a cheque will not command general acceptability as a medium of exchange simply because the payee cannot be certain that it will be met; he has no means of knowing whether there really is any money (deposit) to be transferred. But once the transfer has been effected there is no doubt that the resulting bank deposit will be acceptable in settlement of debts. Thus the limitation on acceptability which attaches to *bank money* derives not from a lack of acceptability of the bank money itself but from a limitation on the part of the mechanism of transfer.

Over a very wide range of transactions this limitation does not operate because the payee possesses knowledge of the credit worth of the person making payment. Where it does exist, however, it is possible to overcome the limitation. This is done by means of bankers' cheques, confirmed credits, and other more recent devices such as the now familiar credit card, which the financial system has invented for rendering the mechanism of transfer of money more efficient.

Before going any further in the clarification of what money is and what is money, it will help to have some idea of the way in which money and the institutions which produce it have evolved. In order to do this we shall use an analytical framework of four stages starting with commodity money. In the second stage we introduce token money and go on to the third and fourth stages in which the significance of the development of banks and other financial institutions will be brought out.

The analysis will be illustrated by reference to the history of development in England, there being no richer record of the development both of monetary institutions and monetary thought than that in the English literature, which is interspersed with a succession of state inquiries into the operations of the system and great controversies surrounding them. No serious student of these matters can afford to be ignorant of the outlines and it is a fascinating field for those who can be tempted to explore it further.

It must be stressed that the stages do not necessarily follow in strict sequence, nor are they mutually exclusive. The distinctions we are going to make are analytical and will therefore over-simplify actual historical events in order to distinguish the significant pattern.

### Stage 1. Commodity Money

Although a great variety of objects have served as a medium of exchange throughout history, there has been a tendency for certain articles to be much more successful than others. If one thinks of the qualities that are required of a medium of exchange it is clear that there are three of particular importance. In the first place the medium of exchange must be limited in supply, for no one would give up goods into which the effort of production had been put in exchange for something like stones which could be acquired by picking them up off the ground. Secondly, it is clearly necessary that the medium should be durable and this links up with the second function of money to which we shall have to give some attention, namely its capacity to act not only as a medium of exchange but as a store of value. Thirdly, it is clear that it is most convenient to have a medium of exchange the unit of which is sufficiently high in value not to require vast quantities for the settlement of normal transactions.

It will be seen that these qualities are possessed *par excellence* by the precious metals, and gold and silver have played the major roles as media of exchange throughout the world, from earliest times.

It may be convenient here to distinguish two sub-stages in the development of commodity money. We can think of the first sub-stage as being that in which the pieces of the commodity, let us call it gold, which are used as money have no distinguishing marks and command goods in exchange by reason of the intrinsic value of the metal from which they are made. In this situation there would be no distinction between the gold handed around as money and the gold used as ornaments. Indeed there was no difference in various parts of Africa, between the cowrie shells which circulated as money and the cowrie shells worn as necklaces. A significant step is taken, however, as soon as some recognizable design or symbol is imposed upon the pieces of gold. If arrangements are made by a monarch or government to mint coins out of gold then, with reservations which we shall need to deal with later, the coins will be accepted by count rather than by weight. As soon as this happens, the possibility emerges of a divergence between the bullion value of the coin and its purchasing power as a unit of currency. This possibility opened up the opportunity of 'debasing the coinage'—an opportunity of which, historically, kings have not been slow to take advantage.

The use of metal coins in England goes back at least to the

8th century before Christ when it is clear that they were accepted by count and not by weight; that is to say the unit which the
coin represented had become a unit of account in its own right.
In Saxon England this unit of account was silver, 1 lb. of which
was equal to the *pound* which still represents the English unit of
account. In William the Conqueror's time it was 240 silver
pennies, weighing 1 lb., which constituted the English unit of
account and this came to be regarded for centuries as 'the
Ancient and Right Standard of England'.[1]

It was not until early in the twelfth century that the unit of
account based on silver came to be referred to as *sterling*—a surprise to many people who associate the word sterling with gold.
Gold coins did, in fact, circulate alongside silver coins in England from as early as 1257 and this complicated the monetary
system a great deal because of the fluctuations in the relative
values of the two metals. These complications of bi-metallism
together with the efforts of successive monarchs, particularly
Henry VIII, to exact funds from the country by debasing the
coinage, constituted the major problems of 'monetary policy'
during the Middle Ages.

By the middle of the eighteenth century it came to be recognized, more by accident than design, that gold had become the
British monetary standard at a value, which persisted until
1931, of £3 17s. 10½d. per standard ounce, eleven-twelfths fine.
At that time the principal gold coin in circulation was the
guinea, which had been introduced in 1663, and after many
vicissitudes had acquired a value of twenty-one shillings, when
it was replaced by the sovereign in 1816. Sovereigns continued
to circulate until 1925, by which time revolutionary changes
had taken place in the medium of exchange involving the introduction of token money and bank money.

## Stage 2. *Token Money*

In the first half of the seventeenth century, the London goldsmiths, whose trade was traffic in coin and bullion, began
to pay interest for deposits of gold or silver coins. The goldsmiths were willing to pay interest because it was, at that time,
profitable either to melt down coin and sell it as bullion when its

[1] Morgan, E. V., *A History of Money*, Penguin Books Ltd., 1965.

purchasing power as coin fell, or to export it when its external value exceeded domestic value. There was also profit to be had from the simple device of sifting the coins deposited with them, paying out the thin ones and melting down the fat ones. It was not long before it became clear that depositors, apart from receiving interest, valued the goldsmiths' services as providing a safe-deposit and the practice soon developed of making payments by handing over the goldsmiths' receipts, instead of going to the goldsmiths and withdrawing the gold, in order to make the payment to someone who, as like as not, would promptly redeposit it with the goldsmiths. As this practice developed, it became clear to the goldsmiths that it was unnecessary to continue operating as a safe-deposit. The more their receipts circulated among their depositors, the more were they able to lend out part of the gold or silver which had been deposited with them. This is the first example in English monetary history of token money resulting from the activities of a financial institution. For that was what had in fact happened: the receipts of the goldsmiths were, as a contemporary phrase put it, 'running current'; that is to say they had become a medium of exchange.

It was not long before others followed the goldsmiths in issuing receipts for deposits. While the goldsmiths confined their activities to London, throughout the whole country small independent country banks were springing up issuing their own notes which, as a result of running current, became part of the circulating medium of the country. Now clearly these receipts for deposits, or *bank notes* as they were coming to be called, were tokens; they had no intrinsic value being simply paper. An important distinction about these tokens at this stage in the development of token money was that they were *representative* tokens which were convertible into a *commodity* money. Thus, although for convenience of payment people would settle their transactions in paper money, these pieces of paper were actually promises to pay gold coin on demand.

This fact had important implications. It meant that the banks issuing them had a liability to meet their notes in gold. This situation in which a token money is convertible on demand into a commodity money, gives rise to the need to hold a reserve of commodity money in order that the bank issuing promises in the form of notes shall always be able to meet its liabilities.

During the great expansion of country banking of the eighteenth and nineteenth centuries in England, the method by which the country banks secured themselves against an excessive demand for repayment of gold was that they, in turn, kept balances with the London banks which had developed into specialist institutions and which in their turn kept balances at the Bank of England. The Bank of England, which had been established by charter in 1694 as a private joint stock company, was itself issuing bank notes, so that during this period, which lasted for two centuries, there were the bank notes of the Bank of England, the bank notes of the London and country bankers, and gold coins, all circulating together; all of the notes, being convertible into gold coin, were representative tokens.

The history of this phase of monetary development in England is not a very happy one. The country banks, being confined to partnerships, operated on a small local scale and were highly unstable. Some indication of the instability of the banking structure at this time is given by the fact that in the first quarter of the nineteenth century 265 country banks went bankrupt.[2]

The significant point to note here is that where a token money is convertible into something of real value, that is to say, into commodity money, there arises the problem of ensuring its convertibility. It was the lack of confidence in the multitude of small banks during the eighteenth and nineteenth centuries which led from time to time to 'runs on the banks' which led the bank in question to draw upon the London banks, which led them in turn to draw upon the Bank of England. In this way the Bank of England came to be the *last resort* of the monetary system and of the London money market, which was developing as specialist financial institutions became established.

It is for these reasons that the history of the Bank of England, during the second half of the eighteenth century and the first half of the nineteenth century, was dominated by the possibility of an internal drain on its gold resources occasioned by lack of confidence in monetary institutions which led depositors to demand actual gold in settlement of notes. This situation persisted until the First World War, except for the period of the restriction on gold payments which operated by law between 1797 and 1819. This period of inconvertible tokens, which co-

[2] Pressnell, L. S., *Country Banking in the Industrial Revolution*, Oxford, 1956.

incided with the French wars, produced one of the first major credit inflations and it was followed by one of the most famous inquiries of the many that have taken place in England into the operation of the monetary system. This inquiry, by a committee appointed by Parliament known as the Bullion Committee, reported in 1810, and their report blamed the inflation upon the excessive issues of bank notes by the Bank of England and the consequential excessive issues by the country banks.

It is not possible to go into the interesting sub-plots of this period or into the involved controversies about the way in which the quantity of money affected the level of prices and the exchange rate. What is important to establish is that it was coming to be recognized that the ability of institutions to issue paper money could have an important effect upon the economic situation and that the question of control of this ability to create money was becoming a matter of public concern. There was at this time, however, no clear recognition by the Directors of the Bank of England that they had a responsibility in this matter. The Bank of England was established as a private enterprise and its function was that of an ordinary bank seeking to maximize the profits of its shareholders. Although the bank, with interruptions and deviations, increasingly realized its public responsibilities, it was not until the Bank of England Act in 1946, that the responsibilities of the Bank of England as a central bank were formally recognized by its nationalization; certainly during the suspension period it was acting simply as a commercial bank which happened to have other commercial banks as its customers.

A recommendation of the Bullion Committee for the resumption of cash payments was not implemented until 1819 when, for the first time, England went on to a fully automatic gold standard with gold sovereigns circulating and bank notes payable in gold on demand. This situation, with slight modifications, continued for a hundred years and the token currency was inter-changeable with gold (except during the First World War and the post-war adjustment period) until 1931. In 1931 Britain abandoned the gold standard in a financial crisis in which the Bank of England was unable to meet the demands for gold from foreign financial centres and therefore had to suspend gold payments as it had done in 1797.

This represents an important stage in monetary development. During the nineteenth century, the Bank had been concerned with two kinds of demand for gold. These were, respectively, the internal drain and the external drain. The internal drain was a reflection of domestic lack of confidence which led from time to time to people demanding gold for internal circulation. By the end of the nineteenth century this had become unimportant—confidence in the token money having been completely established. It was appropriate therefore that, from that time, the arrangement for conversion should relate solely to the demands for external conversion for the purpose of settlement of international payments. A modified form of gold standard, known as the gold bullion standard, was therefore introduced in 1925 by which, although sovereigns continued to circulate, Bank of England notes were only convertible into gold bullion. This very sensible system had a very short life since convertibility into gold at the current exchange rate had to be abandoned in the financial crisis of 1931. The termination of the right to obtain even gold bullion in exchange for Bank of England notes rendered these tokens completely fiduciary. Their direct link with gold of a specified weight and fineness was completely broken and the ultimate step in this development was taken when the entire gold holdings of the Bank of England were transferred, in 1939, to an Exchange Equalization Account, whose function was to intervene in the foreign exchange market to maintain the exchange rate.

One further significant difference between the situation at the beginning of the twentieth century and that at the beginning of the nineteenth century was that by the later period the paper currency consisted entirely of Bank of England notes. This was the result of the provisions of the Bank Charter Act of 1844 which had the effect of gradually eliminating the issues of the private banks.

It will be seen that the history of the development of token currency in England has been a complicated one. This has largely been due to three factors. Firstly, the discrepancy between the face value and the commodity value of coins in circulation. Secondly, the divergence between the commodity values of coins, composed of two different metals, circulating together. And thirdly, the problems arising from the conversion of token money into commodity money where the token money gave the holder an option to demand such conversion.

In the final stage of the development of token currency in England, none of these problems arise. The currency is a pure token and the complications of commodity values and of conversion into commodity money do not arise. In their place, however, there is a new problem. We have already seen that the first experience of issuing token money which was not convertible into commodity money, during the French wars, was associated with considerable inflation. Those countries which are spared the troubles associated with having a currency comprising commodities or convertible into commodities, namely those countries which start their monetary development with a token currency which is entirely fiduciary, are immediately faced with the problem of managing such a currency so as to avoid inflation, and with the need to maintain its external value.

## Stage 3. Deposit Money

We have seen that the goldsmiths and the country bankers in England found it profitable to borrow commodity currency and to issue receipts which began to circulate as a means of payment and that this in itself was a profitable occupation. It was not long, however, before it was realized that, not only was it possible to lend out the actual currency which had been deposited by the depositors, but that it was possible to make loans by means of the notes which were acting as a medium of exchange. The introduction of this important development represents the changeover to modern banking, which entails a change in the role of deposit banks from 'purveyors of money' to 'creators of money'.

In order to see that this is the case let us consider the example of the man who goes into one of the country banks in the nineteenth century and says to the manager that he wishes to borrow £1,000 for the purpose of his business. If the manager is satisfied about the credit-worthiness of the customer, he will agree. The loan can then be effected by handing to the customer £1,000 in the notes of the bank concerned. The successful borrower then goes out and makes his purchases with notes, which are accepted in settlement of debt. What has happened is that the manager's action has had the effect of creating an additional sum of £1,000 in the form of bank notes. So long as these bank notes continue to circulate outside the bank there is in existence £1,000 worth of money which did not exist before. The apparent simplicity of this profitable procedure points the relevance of the strictures of the Bullion Committee upon the excessive issues of bank notes by the Bank of England and, as a consequence, the excessive issues by the country banks. The rules made in the 1844 Bank Charter Act, to control the issue of Bank of England notes, which are still, nominally, a feature of the present British monetary system, derive from the fact that banks, by virtue of the fact that their liabilities circulate as a means of payment, are capable of creating money.

As we have already seen, in England the right to issue notes was gradually taken away from the banks as a result of the 1844 Bank Charter Act. This, however, did not prevent the continuation of the banks' ability to create credit, because the use of cheques as an instrument to transfer deposits between individuals rendered the use of bank notes for this purpose unnecessary. Here we have the final sophistication of the banking system; instead of making loans by handing out their own promissory notes which circulate as a medium of exchange, the banks developed the ultimate refinement of making loans by simply entering figures in their own ledgers. In other words our hypothetical customer going into the modern bank to obtain a loan will not expect to have the loan paid out in the form of bank notes but will simply expect the manager to agree to his drawing cheques on a 'deposit' which has been created in his favour. This deposit is created by a stroke of the pen but, since it can subsequently be transferred by cheques to other people's accounts in settlement of debt, it operates exactly as do bank notes: it is money.

We have now progressed from a situation in which full value commodity currency was used as money to a situation, which is typical of advanced monetary economies, in which the main burden of monetary transactions is borne by a medium of exchange which is evidenced only by figures in books. Moreover it will now be apparent that there is a significant difference between the function which we have just described as being performed by banks in the third stage of our development outline and that which they performed in the second stage when they were simply acting as financial intermediaries channelling savings into the hands of borrowers who spent them. In the third stage they can make new money available to borrowers because their own liabilities have become money.

This is not, of course, a process which can continue without limit, and we shall have to examine the limits on the capacity of the banks to create money in some detail in the next chapter. Here it is sufficient to say that the creation of such *secondary money* depends essentially on the amount of *primary money*, that is to say currency, that the banks can get hold of. This is because of the need to keep a reserve of primary money against the demands by the bank's own customers and the need to settle the claims of other banks.

In the early days of the eighteenth century in England, when the commercial banks were starting to develop, their business consisted of inducing people to deposit currency with them, and this currency formed the basis for an expansion of credit which was some multiple of the currency deposited. Such a secondary expansion of credit can continue so long as people can be induced to go on reducing their currency holdings relative to the volume of their transactions by depositing currency in the banks and using cheques to transfer the bank deposits which they obtain in exchange.

It is significant that at this stage savings which are effected in currency and taken to a bank are not just channelled into productive investment by being lent out by the banks to investors, but in stead enable the banks to make further loans on the basis of their increased holdings of primary money. Whereas in stage one the act of saving necessarily involved an act of hoarding; and in stage two this deflationary bias was just offset by the transfer of the unused purchasing power to the issuer of the token currency by whom it was lent to spenders; in the third stage we have a definite inflationary bias resulting from secondary lending by the banks. It is not perhaps surprising that where all three of these stages of development coexisted in eighteenth century England, the interpretation of monetary events was somewhat confused.

But just as there is a limit to the amount of secondary money that a single bank can create on the basis of a given amount of primary money, so there is a limit to the amount of secondary money which can be created in the whole of the monetary system on the basis of a given amount of primary money. This limit is reached when the amount of currency that the public wish to hold has been reduced to a minimum. When this situation has been reached and the banks have created as much credit as they feel is safe on the basis of their *share* of the primary money, we shall describe the system as being *fully-banked*.

## Stage 4. *The Development of Non-Bank Financial Intermediaries*

This fully-banked situation has obtained in most advanced monetary economies for some time and yet it is still imperfectly understood. Although at this stage there is an efficient and sophisticated banking system, the truth is that we are back in stage one as regards the capacity of the monetary system to make the current savings of surplus units available for expenditure by deficit units.

This statement is so at variance with the apparent facts that it is difficult to grasp. Actually, the argument is quite simple to understand. Let us take an illustration: supposing the reader receives his income by cheque at the beginning of the month and, during January, spends the whole of this income by drawing cheques and thus reduces his balance to zero by the end of the month. Supposing that in February he has been influenced by a thrift campaign and decides to save half of his monthly salary; he will then only draw cheques in respect of an amount equal to half of his salary and his balance will be equal to the other half of his salary, against which he has drawn no cheques, at the end of February. His savings, equal to half a month's salary, are now embodied in his bank deposit. But what is the effect of this on the monetary system? All that he has done by his decision to save is to alter the distribution of deposits as between depositors; he has done nothing whatever which will enable the banks to make any more loans than they were able to make in January.

The parallel with the case of savings embodied in commodity currency is a precise one: bank deposits having become a medium of exchange, the embodiment of savings in the form of bank deposits is the equivalent of hoarding. The only effect of an increase or decrease in saving is a change in the rate at which bank deposits circulate and this has no effect on the capacity of the banking system to make loans at all. We thus, once again, have a deflationary bias built into the monetary system.

Here we are making an analytical division between stages which probably never existed in the actual sequence of monetary development in any country. Before the banking system has got itself fully-banked in the sense we have defined, there tends to be some development of monetary institutions which rectify this defect. Just as financial intermediaries came to the rescue of the system in which commodity money was causing savings to be hoarded, so in the fully-banked situation another layer of financial intermediaries and a capital market come into existence in order to put idle bank money to work.

This results in a great variety of specialist institutions and clarification of their differences and similarities requires the use of a general analytical framework.

The first proposition which needs to be established for this purpose is that all financial institutions are engaged in what has come to be termed *intermediation* in the process of financing deficit expenditure, that is to say expenditure in excess of current income. In particular we shall be concerned with the financing of capital expenditure by firms, but we must not overlook that households too indulge in deficit expenditure and that this too requires finance.

Let us first concentrate on the finance of capital expenditure by firms. One important source for the finance of investment is the firm's own current savings; we shall refer to this as *internal finance* and we note that it does not involve deficit finance nor does it involve any kind of intermediation by a financial institution. The balance sheet change consists solely in an increase in the net worth of the firm in the form of physical assets.

By contrast, any form of external finance involves incurring some kind of liability, the counterpart of which is the flow of credit used to finance the deficit on the part of the spending unit. The simplest form of deficit financing is by the issue of *primary securities* in return for money subscribed by surplus units. The balance sheet effect of this transaction is confined to an increase in liabilities of the firm equal to the deficit expenditure matched on the asset side by an increase in physical assets. The source of finance may be either current savings or a reduction in money balances on the part of the ultimate lender. Such a

direct exchange of money and securities between ultimate
lender and ultimate borrower is reflected in balance sheet
changes only of the lender and borrower and no financial intermediation is involved even though the primary securities may
be disposed of by middle-men in a capital market.

The distinguishing feature of intermediation is that the relationship between the ultimate lender and the ultimate borrower
is an indirect one through a financial institution or institutions,
which thus results in balance sheet effects additional to those of
the borrower and lender. As a result of any financial intermediation there comes into existence additional financial assets and
liabilities equal to the amount of the deficit financed. If instead
of the primary securities being issued directly to the lender they
are issued to the borrower's bank, then the bank's balance sheet
totals increase by the amount of the deficit financed: an increase
in deposit liabilities to the borrower matched by an increase
in its assets in the forms of loans and advances.

The effect would be exactly the same if any other type of
financial intermediary was involved such as a building society, a
finance company, or an insurance company; indeed any lending institution whatever. The only feature which is peculiar
when the transaction is with a bank is that, in that case, the
particular financial asset created functions as the generally
accepted means of payment; it is money. In the case of all other
financial institutions, the financial assets created, though they
may be almost indistinguishable from money as assets, have to
be changed into money in order to make payments.

We can thus define intermediation as 'the purchase of primary securities from ultimate borrowers and the issue of *indirect
debt* for the portfolio of ultimate lenders'.[3] Between the ultimate
borrowers and the ultimate lenders there may be more or less
intermediation according to the sophistication of the financial
system. Thus, if the ultimate borrower issues securities directly
to the ultimate lender there is no indirect debt created and the
coefficient measuring the ratio of the total increase in financial
assets to the deficit which is being financed is zero. If there is
one financial institution involved there will be an equal amount
of indirect debt created, giving rise to a total increase in finan-

[3] Gurley, J. G., and Shaw, E. S., *Money in a Theory of Finance*, Washington D.C.,
1960.

cial assets equal to the amount of the deficit financed. The co-efficient in that case is one. There may, however, be more than one stage of intermediation. Insurance companies, which issue a great variety of indirect debt in exchange for money obtained from ultimate savers, buy indirect debt in the form of Unit Trust securities, the issuers of which buy the primary securities of the ultimate spenders. Here the coefficient would be two. A wider concept including primary securities can be expressed in respect of the total stock of wealth and the total value of financial assets at any point in time. This ratio can be taken as a measure of the intensity of financial interrelationships within the economy and, because such intensity is highly corre-lated with specialization and economies of scale, it can be taken as an index of financial development. The ratio has been termed the *financial interrelations ratio* (FIR) by Goldsmith whose study for the O.E.C.D. Development Centre calculated FIR for a number of countries.[4]

The ratio ranged from 1·70 (UK) to 0·65 (France) among developed countries and from 0·40 (Mexico) to 0·15 (Ethiopia) among less developed countries. The very high figure for the United Kingdom (1·70) compared with 1·25 for the United States was largely due to the exceptionally high level of govern-ment debt. Ten years later the figure for the United Kingdom calculated by the authors for 1976 had fallen to about unity, national debt having fallen from 60 to 34 per cent of G.N.P.

The conventional measure of intermediation (a flow concept, as distinct from the FIR stock concept) is the *financial savings ratio*. This is defined as the total annual net increment in financial assets of all financial intermediaries ($\Delta FAi$) divided by savings of the same period. The denominator differs from the total indirect debt instruments (to which the coefficient discussed above applies) by the amount of 'layering' at succes-sive stages within the financial system. For the United Kingdom it is about 0·45 and Table 1 shows the frequency distribution of this ratio for developed and developing countries.

The lower mode (0·2 to 0·3) in the bi-modal distribution of the developed countries mainly relates to countries in which the share of the capital market in total financial sector financing

4 Goldsmith, R. W., The Determinants of Financial Structure O.E.C.D. Development Centre, Paris, 1966.

## Table 1

*Financial Savings Ratio*

| $\dfrac{\Delta FAi}{s}$ | Developed Countries per cent of total | Developing Countries per cent of total |
|---|---|---|
| Over 0·5 | 4 | 3 |
| 0·4 to 0·5 | 31 | 5 |
| 0·3 to 0·4 | 15 | 6 |
| 0·2 to 0·3 | 31 | 18 |
| 0·1 to 0·2 | 15 | 54 |
| Below 0·1 | 4 | 14 |

is high relative to that of financial institutions; the United States falls within this bracket with a ratio of 0·29. In developing countries the general absence of formal capital markets makes this element insignificant.

Although the exposition in this quasi-historical introduction has been in terms of 'flows of surpluses' into 'financing of deficit expenditure', the transition to credit creation allows the process of intermediation to be defined (as in the Gurley and Shaw definition) without implication as to the direction of causation of the increase in indirect debt instruments. Indeed it is more in keeping with post-Keynesian analysis, with its emphasis on the primacy of expenditure, to regard financial intermediaries as financing deficit expenditure in response to demand for credit and, in so doing, creating financial assets the net total of which must be absorbed in private sector holdings as *ex post* savings. The willingness of the public to absorb them lies at the heart of monetary theory.

# II

## MONEY AND THE CREDIT BASE

THE purpose of this chapter is to investigate the basic relationships between the different levels of money and credit by means of a general model which is applicable to any monetary system despite specific institutional differences.

We define as primary money those assets which constitute the ultimate means of payment as distinct from secondary money which is a claim to primary money. Generally primary money is the liability of the monetary authority which is normally a *central bank*. In most countries primary money consists of coin, the central bank's notes and the balances which the banks keep with the central bank. With the exception of coin (which can be disregarded for the purpose of monetary analysis in developed economies) primary money therefore consists of liabilities of the central bank in the form of notes and deposits. The former are held by the public and by the banks while the latter are held exclusively by the banks.

These liabilities, which are the primary money of our general model, we shall call *cash*. The secondary money of the model comprises such deposit liabilities of financial institutions as operate as a medium of exchange in effecting payments, a criterion which is discussed later in this chapter. These *bank deposits* are claims to cash which the public can exercise at its discretion.

Since primary and secondary money are interchangeable at the option of the public, a bank must always hold a stock of cash with which to meet an excess of encashments over cash deposits by its customers. We shall refer to the difference between these two items as the *encashment balance*. In addition, in a multi-bank system, it must hold a stock of cash out of which to meet any excess of claims by other banks over claims against them; that is to say an excess of cheque payments by its own customers over their cheque receipts. This balance is established daily by a process of offsetting cheques at the bankers' clearing house and is then settled by drawing on the debtor banker's balance at the central bank; we shall refer to this as the *clearing balance*.

The effect of a negative encashment balance is a fall in the notes and coins held in the tills and vaults of the bank; the effect of a negative clearing balance is a fall in the bank's balance with the central bank. Since banks in most countries regard balances at the central bank as equivalent to coin and notes (into which they are always instantly convertible), the problem of adjusting the relative magnitudes of the two elements in banks' cash reduces to an administrative problem without monetary significance. For our purpose it is only the total which matters, and we conclude therefore that the banker must hold cash in one or other of these forms to provide for the possibility of the clearing and encashment balances, taken together, being negative.

We next come to the question of how much he must hold. This may be determined by experience, convention, or law. In most countries the central bank has power to specify and vary the *minimum reserve ratio* between specified reserve assets and deposit liabilities. Generally cash is specified; hence primary money (currency plus the deposits of the commercial banks with the central bank) is termed *reserve money* or, for reasons which follow, *high powered money*. Since 1971, the United Kingdom minimum reserve ratio has been specified as liquid assets comprising cash plus certain short-term securities. This does not alter the fact that primary money is the ultimate base of the system and corresponds with the operational liabilities of the monetary authority, thus providing the most effective control fulcrum in a way which will now be demonstrated. The minimum cash ratio requires that:

$$D \leqq \frac{1}{\beta} C_b \qquad (1)$$

where $\beta$ is the banks' cash ratio, $D$ is deposits and $C_b$ is the banks' cash. We shall first make the simplifying assumption that an increase in deposits will not lead to any increase in the amount of cash required by the public. This means that the banker can increase deposits, by buying securities and making advances, without any permanent loss of cash through the encashment balance. On this assumption, the banker passively receiving an additional cash deposit can actively increase deposits by an amount equal to the increase in cash multiplied by the reciprocal of the cash ratio. Using $\Delta$ to indicate increments of deposits and cash we may, therefore, write:

$$\Delta D = \frac{1}{\beta} \Delta C_b \qquad (2)$$

That this equation holds for the system comprising only one bank is obvious, since a single bank cannot lose cash through the clearing balance (there is none), and we are assuming, for the moment, that it does not lose cash through the encashment balance. On receiving additional cash, a monopoly banker can increase his loans (and therefore his deposits) by an amount bearing the same ratio to the additional cash as his existing deposits bear to his existing cash, namely $\beta$.

On the same assumption regarding encashments, the equation holds equally for the multi-bank system as a whole, but in that case the final result is achieved as the product of a series of steps. Each individual step corresponds with the description of his business which is contained in the banker's argument that he does not 'create' deposits but simply lends money which has been deposited with him. Indeed, in view of the necessity of keeping a constant ratio between cash and deposits, he is able to lend only $1 - \beta$ times any additional cash he obtains. What the banker's argument does not recognize is that, even if it is assumed that the whole of any additional loans are lost at the clearing (the assumption made here), the cash lost would simply be transferred to another bank, where it would again constitute the basis for expansion. This process will go on until the drain of cash into bank tills resulting from the necessity to keep back part of any cash gain has exhausted the whole of the initial increase in cash. At each stage of expansion total deposits increase by a gradually diminishing amount until the limiting value is reached. The expansion thus takes the form:

$$\Delta D = \Delta C_b + (1 - \beta) \Delta C_b + (1 - \beta)^2 \Delta C_b \ldots + (1 - \beta)^n \Delta C_b$$

which approaches the limit $\dfrac{\Delta C_b}{\beta}$ as in equation (2) above.

Thus, as in the case of the single bank system, the volume of deposits which any number of banks create on the basis of an initial increase in their cash is a multiple of that increase in cash, and the multiplier is given by the reciprocal of the cash ratio. We shall call this the *bank multiplier*.

So far we have assumed that the public keeps its holding of cash constant while its deposits are increasing and that, as a result, there is no loss of cash by encashment. This assumption is unrealistic and must now be removed. We approach nearer to reality if we assume that in normal circumstances the members of the public, like the banks, arrange their assets so that cash bears some fairly constant ratio to deposits. We shall call this the *public's cash ratio*. Since it is a behavioural variable dependent on the rate of interest and income level, it is not, of course, nearly so rigid as the banks' cash ratio, but for the moment it will be assumed to be constant. We shall write this ratio as $\alpha$.

From this relation it follows that there must be a drain of cash out of the banks as deposits increase, since the public seeks to keep the ratio of cash to deposits constant. This encashment drain must therefore be added to the drain into the tills of the banks which we have already examined. At each step in the process of expansion the amount of banks' cash which is surplus to the requirement of the cash ratio becomes reduced, not simply by $\beta$ times the increase in deposits but by $\alpha + \beta$ times this increase. Thus, when we take this factor into consideration, equation (2) must be replaced by:

$$\Delta D = \frac{1}{\alpha + \beta} \Delta C. \tag{3}$$

And since total money equals $D + Cp$

$$\Delta M = \left(\frac{1 + \alpha}{\alpha + \beta}\right) \Delta C. \tag{4}$$

In behavioural terms this model represents the constraint within which banks can expand, in response to demand, weighing risk against the loss of profit entailed in accumulating excess reserves. Alternatively equations (3) and (4) can be regarded as coefficients of expansion since *ex post* these equations show the relationship which must necessarily exist between primary money and secondary money, and are nothing more than convenient arrangements of the data. They do not imply anything concerning the direction of causation and they are consistent either with cash being adjusted to deposits or with deposits being adjusted to cash. These matters will be discussed in a later chapter.

The above relationship between total deposits of residents and cash is shown in Figure II.1 in which $\alpha$ and $\alpha + \beta$ are reflected in the two vectors, the cash base being equal to the operational liabilities of central bank matched by domestic assets $(DA)$ and foreign assets $(FA)$. For a given cash base the level of deposits is determined by $\alpha$ and $\beta$, and if these ratios were constant over time it would be possible to deduce the total of deposits for any value of the cash base by applying a constant coefficient of expansion. In fact this is not the case with $\alpha$, which is a behavioural variable determined by income and

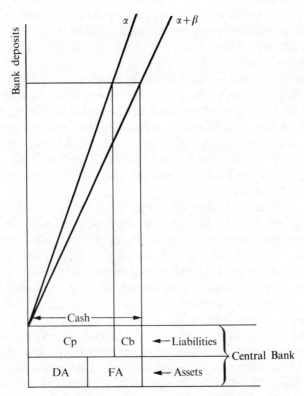

Fig. II.1. Relationship between Cash and Bank Deposits

interest rate. But this does not inhibit control of $C_b$ because the authorities can compensate for variations in $C_p$. More important is the degree to which the banks can induce the public to reduce their holdings of currency relative to deposits.

In the long run the banks can clearly influence the public's monetary habits by offering extended services and by advertising. But can they, in the short run, increase their own holding of cash at the public's expense? Clearly they would have to increase the compensation given to the public, and if they are already giving the maximum service this would mean paying higher interest on deposits. Even if such interest payments as the bank could afford were effective, however, their gain in cash could be offset by the action of the monetary authorities in contracting the total supply of cash. In general we can think of the monetary authorities as allowing total cash to expand and contract to satisfy the demand of the public as to how it wishes to hold its money, but not allowing this (unless the authorities so desire) to affect the banks' cash base, just as they do with seasonal variations.

The major conclusion derived from the above analysis is that, assuming excess reserves to be zero (not unlikely in a situation in which there is need for constraint), there is a definite, though not rigid, multiple relationship between the stock of money as a whole and the liabilities of the central bank. So long, therefore, as the central bank can control its own liabilities it can control, broadly, the total stock of money, and we must now examine how this is done.

In general a central bank which has sole issue of primary money can vary its liabilities by buying and selling financial assets in the open market. Since it uses primary money for these transactions, the cash base changes by an equal amount. Thus the sale of an asset by the central bank must reduce primary money by a like amount, no matter who buys the asset. If the sale is made to a member of the public, he will pay by drawing on a commercial bank in favour of the central bank; if the sale is to a commercial bank, that bank will draw on its balance with the central bank in favour of the central bank. The result, in both cases, is that the commercial banks' balances at the central bank are reduced. As we have seen, these balances are regarded by the banks as cash and are therefore part of the cash base.

Such sales and purchases undertaken by the central bank at its own initiative are known as *open-market operations* and there can be no doubt that any central bank can perform such transactions so long as there is a ready market in which to operate and it is willing to take the consequences. The latter condition we shall return to in the final chapter in discussing monetary policy.

As an alternative to control being exercised in the market by variation of $C$, the same result can be obtained by variation of $\beta$. An increase in the minimum cash ratio to above the existing ratio will cause a contraction in bank lending, thus reducing the money supply. Whether or not a decrease in the minimum ratio to below the existing ratio will induce an expansion of bank lending will depend (*a*) on potential demand and (*b*) on the profit/risk relationship. Expansion is most likely if the central bank is responding to an increase in demand for credit; it is less likely if it is trying to stimulate demand.

Similar in principle to variation in the minimum cash ratio is the device by which the central bank calls for, or releases, *special deposits*. When the banks are required to deposit specified amounts of special deposits with the central bank this sterilizes an equal amount of banks' cash causing contraction. The results of a call or release of special deposits are thus identical with the results of an increase or decrease in the minimum cash ratio. In the same category of controls, most central banks also have powers to impose ceilings on bank credit expansion by directives to the banks.

The method of control to which most attention has been given in the literature is that of *open-market operations*, but in countries in which the financial system lacks an effective market (the majority of the developing countries), control of the supply of money is confined to variation of $\beta$, special deposits and directives. Even in fully developed financial systems the non-market types of control are frequently used.

One further important question which must be raised is whether these constraints can be frustrated by operations undertaken by the financial institutions or the government. This involves consideration of central banks' function as the *lender of last resort* to the financial system and to the government.

The basic responsibility of the central bank to financial

institutions is that of ensuring their financial viability in a crisis, but, more generally, provision is normally made to overcome transitory shortages of cash in order to maintain stability. That this latter practice does not inhibit control of the cash base is due to the fact that the central bank can determine the rate of interest at which this support is given. This *Bank Rate* (which may be a rate of discount on bills purchased or a rate of interest on a loan) is normally kept above the marginal rate of interest at which the financial institution can lend. It is therefore a penal rate involving borrowers in an excess of marginal cost over marginal revenue which will induce them to contract in order to minimize losses.

The responsibility of lender of last resort to the government is that of ensuring that the government has the necessary money to cover any gap between public sector revenue and expenditure. The residual is the *public sector borrowing requirement* (*PSBR*), which must be financed by borrowing. One element in financing this deficit is borrowing from the central bank, and when this finance is drawn upon to make payments to the private sector it increases the cash base. It is this credit extended to government which constitutes the domestic assets of the central bank (*DA* in Figure II.1), in the general case in which it lends only to the government.

Finally the control of the cash base requires that the central bank can offset the exogenous effects of the over-all balance of foreign payments and receipts, a surplus in which will increase (and a deficit decrease) the foreign assets (*FA* in Figure II.1).

It is convenient at this point to make a distinction between an increase in the money supply ($\Delta M$) and the concept of *domestic credit expansion* (*DCE*). The words 'domestic credit' are somewhat misleading because *DCE* refers only to domestic monetary expansion, being equal to the increase in the domestic assets of the banks whose liabilities are money. In a closed economy $\Delta M = DCE$ and this is also the case if the over-all balance of payments is exactly in balance, leaving the foreign assets of the central bank unchanged: $\Delta FA = O$. However, if during the period over which $\Delta M$ is measured, $\Delta FA$ is positive, $\Delta M$ will be greater than *DCE*, and if $\Delta FA$ is negative, $\Delta M$ will be less than *DCE*. Thus *DCE* is the correct measure for total domestic monetary credit expansion and $\Delta M$ is the correct measure of the sum of the monetary assets thus created which is added to domestic portfolios.

The relationship we have set out above in respect of the money stock and the banking system which creates it are not unique, they are reproduced in essentials in respect of the non-bank financial intermediaries which form the next 'layer' in the financial system. They too create credit and thus finance deficit expenditure on the part of the ultimate borrower; they too need to keep reserves in the form of assets into which their liabilities are convertible; they too can be regarded as generating a multiple expansion of credit the limiting factor in which is (as with the banks) the quantity of *reserve assets* they can get hold of. But in this case, the reserve assets are the deposits of the banking sector; they are secondary money, not primary.

The equation showing the significant relationships is as follows:

$$F = \frac{1}{\gamma + \delta}\left(\frac{C}{\alpha + \beta}\right)$$

where $F$ is assets of non-bank intermediaries; $\gamma$ the desired ratio $\frac{D_p}{F}$; $\delta$ the desired ratio $\frac{D_f}{F}$; $D_f$ the intermediaries' reserve bank balances; $D_p$ the public's deposits in banks. Since $\frac{C}{\alpha + \beta} = D$, we have $\frac{1}{\gamma + \delta}$ as the multiplier based on a change in deposits, assuming both ratios constant.

Alternatively, if we suppose that bank deposits remain unchanged but that there is a once and for all shift in bank deposits to financial intermediaries with the marginal ratio remaining constant, the effect of such a shift in deposits is given by

$$\Delta F = \frac{1}{\delta}\,\Delta D_f.$$

Finally, suppose that there is a fall in the ratio $\frac{D_f}{F}$ from $\delta$ to $\delta'$. Assuming that $\alpha + \beta$ remains unchanged, this will give rise to an initial transfer of bank deposits from the public to non-bank intermediaries; this (except for money reserves retained by the latter) will be lent out thus starting the normal multiplier sequence, the increment in assets of intermediaries being given by

$$\Delta F = \frac{\delta - \delta'}{(\gamma + \delta')(\gamma + \delta)} \, \Delta D.$$

In no case does the volume of money alter as a result of the activities of intermediaries—its velocity increases as debt increases. Moreover, financial intermediaries are not peculiar in sharing with banks this credit-creating expansionary characteristic; on similar assumptions the same analysis could be applied to a further layer of trade credit, but the values of the multipliers would only be meaningful if the ratios were constant.

This multiplier approach to the credit structure has the merit of reflecting the dependence of the whole inverted pyramid of credit on primary money. Its defect is that it gives too rigid and simplistic a picture of the relationship between balance sheets contained in the more behavioural portfolio balance approach. There is, however, no contradiction between the two approaches,[1] and the treatment of money as simply one of the range of financial assets tends to detract from its unique function as a means of payment.

Identification of this unique asset has long been the subject of controversy and we must now deal with the extreme view on this matter as revealed in a well known proposition advanced by Professor R. S. Sayers that '. . . there is no single asset or group of assets that uniquely possesses a uniform monetary quality that is totally absent from all other assets'.[2] It will be contended that this proposition neglects the essential characteristic of money and that when this characteristic is given its correct significance the proposition is not true.

As Professor Sayers himself says, 'the difficulty of identification has derived from the two-fold nature of money as a medium of exchange and as a store of value'. It is the present contention that Sayers's failure to identify money results from his failure correctly to apply the criteria relating to the former function. If we look at the status of assets as a store of value from the point of view of the owner, the monetary quality consists in

---

[1] See Goodhart, C. A. E., *Money Information and Uncertainty*, London, 1975.

[2] Sayers, R. S., 'Monetary Thought and Monetary Policy in England', *Economic Journal*, December 1960.

the ability to exercise the purchasing power which the assets represent, by right, without penalty or delay. It is this criterion which has been the basis of most of the 'perennial questions of controversy' and which involves the hair-splitting, which Sayers finds so unsatisfactory in distinguishing between money and non-money. On the basis of the foregoing criteria we should include as money: current accounts but not deposit accounts; Post Office Savings Bank accounts up to the 'on demand' limit but not the rest; demand deposits in Building Societies but not time deposits; indeed, any form of call loan but not any period loan. It will be generally agreed that such distinctions are of negligible significance in monetary analysis; but if they are abandoned where do we stop? The answer surely is that we cannot stop. Financial assets, looked at from this point of view, constitute a class within which the individual components are differentiated only by the point in time at which they possess the characteristic of entitling the owner to means of payment.

This being so, we draw the line according to the purpose which we have in mind, and no class of assets which we choose to distinguish will possess a uniform monetary quality that is totally absent from all other assets. It is to the exchange function that we must turn if we are to identify this quality.

Sayers dismisses the medium of exchange criterion as follows: 'The usual answer is that we should include as money only those assets which are commonly used as media of exchange. Resort to the adverb "commonly" at once emphasizes the absence of any sharp line of distinction.' It is the basis of the present argument that this is not the case if the line of distinction is correctly specified in terms of operational effects in the economy rather than according to asset status from the point of view of the owner.

The analytical distinction we wish to draw in the money/non-money classification is clearly exemplified in the distinction between currency and bonds. Currency (being commonly used as a medium of exchange) changes hands physically in making a payment, and this involves no repercussion in the economy whatever. Bonds, on the other hand, not being commonly used as a medium of exchange, can only be drawn upon to finance a payment by recourse to the bond market.

We have now to generalize this distinction. An asset can only be regarded as a means of payment if the effect of drawing upon it to make a payment is identical with the effect of a physical transfer of currency. That is to say, the effects outside the banking sector must be confined to the change in the indebtedness between payer and payee. This will be the case only if the consequential adjustments in the banking sector have a zero sum. When this is so the payment will not involve any change in the asset/liability complex of the public other than that between the payer and the payee; such a payment will be termed *neutral*.

When this neutrality condition is not satisfied the non-zero sum of the consequential financial transactions must involve an effect in the market for loans which could not attach to the transfer of a medium of exchange *simpliciter*. This effect may take either of two forms: (i) the sale of an asset by the person making the payment; or (ii) a draft on the payers' claims by a financial intermediary, involving a reduction in the aggregate of such claims and a consequential sale of an asset by the intermediary. The nature of the first case is obvious; we shall be concerned with the second case.

Bank deposits subject to transfer by cheque have long been treated as means of payment, in spite of the fact that their use does not involve a simple transfer between payer and payee. In fact, payment by cheque involves at least three elements:

1. a reduction in the payer's deposit;
2. a transfer of cash from the payer's bank to the payee's bank;
3. an increase in the payee's deposit.

The treatment of this process as equivalent to a transfer *simpliciter* is justified on the neutrality criterion by the well-established fact that in a developed banking system the consequential financial transactions have a zero sum either because the banks have homogeneous reserve conventions or they have an internal market in bank funds.

But there has always been a class of assets (generally known as *quasi-money*) whose classification has been ambiguous. This ambiguity is due to the fact that the question as to which assets are properly classed as money has been dominated by consideration of the status of assets as a store of value from the point of view of the owner, to the neglect of the functional criterion. Consider the following questions: can a line be drawn between current accounts and deposit accounts? Are balances in the Post Office Savings Bank money? Are demand deposits in a Building Society any different from clearing-bank deposits? What about unused overdraft facilities? If we answer these questions with reference to the store of value status of the asset from the owner's point of view we shall split hairs which are of no real significance in monetary analysis and ignore the really significant distinction which is revealed by the neutrality criterion. Let us apply this criterion to the above questions.

On this basis the first question is an easy one. The answer is that deposit accounts should be classified with current accounts in the United Kingdom because the banks do not distinguish between them in their liquidity conventions. A payment made with a cheque on a deposit account and credited to a current account leaves the total of deposits in equilibrium at an unchanged level, and thus has no repercussions in the market for loans. Although the status of the asset acquired is not identical with that given up, the practical distinction in the United Kingdom is insignificant in monetary analysis.

In banking systems where the banks differentiate in their liquidity conventions between deposit accounts and current accounts (using the English terms for convenience) the classification of the former as money would render analysis inaccurate to the extent that payments made from them would not be neutral. Correct analysis would require that the operation should be decomposed into its two elements: (i) the conversion of the deposit account into current account (involving a repercussion in the loan market); and (ii) the transfer of the current account deposit (which is neutral in its effects) to the payee. The same applies to all non-bank financial intermediaries.

The currently accepted answer to the question about unused overdraft facilities follows Keynes's *Treatise*[3] in including them in money. Once again, however, this is the result of looking at the status of the asset from the point of view of the owner; on the functional criterion such facilities cannot be regarded as money, for the simple reason that any net use made of them could not be neutral. Given the banks' liquidity conventions,

[3] Keynes, J. M., *Treatise on Money*, London, 1933, Vol. II, pp. 42-3.

net increase in the use of overdraft facilities must necessitate a reduction in some other asset (e.g. securities), and thus involve a repercussion in the market for loans and a net reduction in the class of assets which includes both deposits and unused overdraft facilities.

This approach does seem to give watertight reasons for distinguishing between money (assets which operate like a medium of exchange in making payments) and quasi-money (assets which have virtually the same characteristics as money as a store of value but do not operate like a medium of exchange). It is not claimed that this analysis entirely disposes of the problem of identification but that the problem which remains is institutional, not theoretical, and must be approximated in the context of any particular piece of analysis. There may be actual instances where P.O.S.B. or Building Society deposits are transferred in making payment, just as there may be instances where bonds are so transferred, but for purposes of analysis these instances are insignificant.

It has been argued that this criterion is not valid because when bonds are drawn on to make a payment the person receiving the payment may buy bonds, and the effect would then be the same as if bonds had changed hands. It is true that this could happen but it is not the *necessary* consequence of the payment. Neither is it correct that the non-neutrality of *encashment* of deposits refutes the criterion which correctly relates both to payments by deposits and by currency.[4] If the set of transactions effecting the payment is exactly equivalent to a hand-to-hand transfer of currency the asset which was drawn upon to finance the payment can be regarded as money.

In general equilibrium terms we define money as consisting of those assets the use of which by the owner to finance an excess demand in the market for commodities or factors of production, necessarily has zero effect in the market for loans. In terms of our previous analysis of deficit finance, money is the only asset the possession of which enables spending units to finance deficits

---

[4] This argument by Friedman, M., and Schwartz, A., in 'The Definition of Money', *Journal of Money, Credit and Banking*, vol. i, no. i, 1971, is refuted in the same Journal, Newlyn, W. T., vol. ii, no. i, 1972, but is cited uncritically by Goodhart, C. A. E., *Money Information and Uncertainty*, London, 1975.

without recourse to a market or intermediation. Its unique character is further delineated by the following:

1. Its possession is necessary for making any payment.
2. In particular it is exclusively used in payment for services of factors of production.
3. As a corollary it is the asset in which all incomes are received.
4. As a further corollary it is the asset the holding of which automatically rises and falls with receipts and expenditure and is thus the asset in which surpluses are embodied in the absence of purchase of another financial asset.

The problem of the actual identification of a unique value for money stock can be illustrated by reference to the financial institutions of the United Kingdom. Two aggregates are designated by the Bank of England as money: a 'narrow' and a 'broad' concept known respectively as M1 and M3 (the intermediate M2 having been discarded). M1 consists of notes and coin held by the public plus sterling current accounts of the United Kingdom private sector with *banks*.[5] The broad version, M3, includes in addition sterling deposit accounts, accounts denominated in foreign currencies, and accounts of the public sector. The magnitude of M3 has tended to be about twice that of M1. Neither includes the sterling deposits of overseas residents, this being justified by the argument that 'changes in such balances may reflect international capital movements whose causes may not be very closely connected with developments in the United Kingdom economy'.[6]

Following the changes introduced in 1971, the reserve requirements have been uniform for all banks and they are therefore the set of financial intermediaries in respect of which the neutrality criterion applies. Furthermore, since the reserve requirement does not discriminate as to type of deposit, it is M3 which corresponds with the theoretical specification based on the neutrality of a financial asset as a means of payment.

This definition of money according to its function as a means of payment in no way excludes an entirely different categoriza-

---

[5] These include the London and Scottish Clearing Banks, Northern Ireland banks, other deposit banks, accepting houses, and branches of overseas banks.

[6] Deputy Governor of Bank of England, a speech reproduced in *Bank of England Quarterly Bulletin*, June 1973.

tion of the range of debt instruments as *assets*. Here the only criterion is homogeneity of sub-sets with respect to holder's preference. Within bank deposits there would clearly be two distinct sub-sets in respect of zero or positive interest yield. But for the identification of other sub-sets let econometric analysis decide.

International comparability is clearly complicated by these considerations, but the International Monetary Fund's designation of the narrow aggregate as money, and the additional items in the broad aggregate as *quasi money* goes as far as is possible to providing a standard international definition.

# III

## WHY MONEY IS HELD

In this chapter it is proposed to explore the question as to why people hold money in the light of its dual function as a means of payment and as a store of wealth. It is appropriate therefore to start with the celebrated Keynesian classification of the motives for holding money which covers both functions. This approach via motives is, in the writers' view, still entirely comprehensive and proof against the criticism made of it, if correctly interpreted.[1] Keynes classified the motives for holding money under three heads: the transactions motive; the precautionary motive; and the speculative motive. The explanation of each is given below in his own words (seldom done in text books) but with his second motive divided into two elements which will be treated separately in the present analysis.[2]

1. Transactions motive: '... the need of cash for the current transactions of personal and business expenditure.'
2. Precautionary motive: (i) 'to provide for contingencies requiring sudden expenditure and for unforeseen opportunities of advantageous purchase, *and also* (ii) to hold an asset of which the value is fixed in terms of money.'
3. Speculative motive: 'the object of securing profit from knowing better than the market what the future will bring forth.'

The term 'cash' in 1 is equivalent to money in the present analysis. The emphasis in 2 is added by the present writers as the

---

[1] Two additional motives have been cited: (i) the deflation motive (Day, A. C., *Outline of Monetary Economics*, Oxford, 1957) and (ii) the diversification motive (Gurley, J. G., and Shaw, E. S., *Money in a Theory of Finance*, Washington D.C., 1960). (i) which is associated with an expectation of falling prices is not strictly a motive for holding money since bonds are a preferred alternative *cet. par.* if expectations change in this respect. (ii) which is associated with spreading risks is covered by the precautionary motive. But Gurley and Shaw's approach via portfolio balance is a valid alternative approach to that via Keynes's three motives.

[2] Keynes, J. M., *The General Theory of Employment, Interest and Money*, London, 1936, pp. 196 and 170.

double conjunction gives strong support to the partial separation of these two elements.

With this general and comprehensive approach to the reasons
for holding money we turn first to consider in detail the transactions motive which derives from the means of payment function.

### I. *Money as a Means of Payment*

In order to consider the holding of money as a means of payment we shall classify money, according to its actual behaviour,
into *active* and *idle*.[3]

As generally used in monetary theory these terms require
special interpretation; activity in this context refers to transactions which generate income; transactions which simply
represent an exchange of assets do not, for this purpose, constitute activity. Thus, money which is changing hands in Stock
Exchange transactions, for example, is regarded as idle because
it is not active in the sense of generating income. Throughout
this chapter, however, we shall assume that no such financial
transactions take place, so that the pattern of money balances is
determined exclusively by the income-generating activity of
money. This artificial separation will enable us to concentrate
in the present chapter on those factors which affect the total requirement for means of payment associated with any particular
level of income in a given institutional context.

At any point of time all money is idle, just as all moving objects are motionless in an instantaneous photograph, so that it is
clearly necessary to introduce a time element in order to define
idleness and activity. Any individual or firm engaging in monetary transactions may be represented as receiving and paying
out money in some more or less regular pattern. These periodic
receipts and payments will impose upon the money balance a
more or less regular time shape, the money balance rising and
falling with the receipts and payments. It is this time shape of
the money balance which enables us to distinguish between
active and idle money in the sense in which those terms are here
used.

The division will be clear from an inspection of the highly

---

[3] Angell, J. W., 'The Components of the Circular Velocity of Money', *Quarterly
Journal of Economics*, February 1937.

simplified diagram in Figure III.1. Idle money is simply that part of his money balance into which the individual does not need to dip in the course of his normally recurring transactions, that is to say, his minimum balance; active money is the average

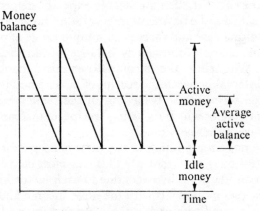

Fig. III.1. Active and Idle Money

value of the fluctuating component, that is to say, his average holding in excess of his minimum balance.

We have now to establish the factors which determine the average level of active money. For the individual, given the level of income, these factors are the *time-pattern of expenditure* and the *payments interval* which together determine the *income-expenditure period*.[4] These terms must now be explained.

The time shape of the money balance of any individual or firm engaging in continuous economic activity will show regularly recurring maxima, the interval between which will be determined by the frequency of the regularly recurring payments and receipts. The interval between succeeding maxima is called the payments interval. For an individual wage or salary earner the payments interval would be the interval between wage or salary receipts, which might be a week or a month; for a retail store the interval might be that between quarter-days,

[4] Angell, J. W., op. cit., and Ellis, H. S., 'Some Fundamentals in the Theory of Velocity', *Quarterly Journal of Economics*, May 1938, reprinted in *Readings in Monetary Theory*, London, 1952.

when payments are made to wholesalers; for some agricultural undertakings the interval might be as long as a year.

Now if all payments into the account within the payments interval were received together, and if all the money received were retained throughout the entire payments interval and spent at the end of it, then the income-expenditure period would be identical with the payments interval; this, however, is clearly only a limiting case and there is an infinite range of possibilities of the time shape of the money balance within the payments interval. We define the income-expenditure period as the average interval between the receipt of income and its expenditure, or, in terms of the behaviour of the money balance, the average period for which recurring receipts of income remain in the balance of the individual.

We are now in a position to use these concepts for analysing the active money requirement. This can most conveniently be done by considering differences due to each factor in turn. We take, first, two individuals with the same income and the same pattern of expenditure within the payments interval, but with different payments intervals; individuals for whom, therefore, the income-expenditure period is different. The time shape of the money balances of two such individuals is shown in Figure III.2(a).

The continuous line indicates the time shape of the money balance of an individual who receives his income monthly, while the broken line indicates that of an individual who receives the same annual income weekly. The income-expenditure period of the first is two weeks while that of the second is half a week; the average active balance of the first is four times that of the second. This difference occurs with an identical pattern of expenditure because of the difference in the payments interval.

The income-expenditure period, and therefore the money requirements, will also vary with differences in the pattern of expenditure for any given payments interval. This is shown in Figure III.2(b). Here the payments intervals are identical but the income-expenditure periods differ because of different expenditure patterns. The expenditure pattern represented by the continuous line gives an income-expenditure period of two weeks, but that for the broken line is only one week. The aver-

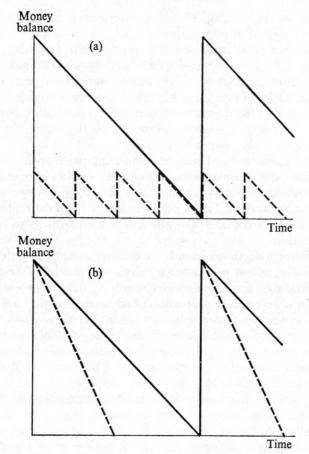

FIG. III.2. (a). Payment-Interval Effect. (b). Payment-Pattern Effect

age active balance in the first case is twice that in the second case.

Thus the average level of active money for the individual or firm is seen to depend on the length of the income-expenditure period, and the latter to depend on the expenditure pattern and the payments interval.

For the economy as a whole the overlapping of stages in the production process necessitates additional holdings ranging between a maximum and minimum determined by the maximum payments interval and the sum of the payments intervals of the several stages, with the intermediate case half-way between these limits in both respects.[5]

The factors determining the relationship between active money and income we shall refer to as the *payment complex*. They are institutional factors which, in the short period, and under normal circumstances, can be regarded as stable. Within these limits we should, therefore, have a stable relationship between active money requirement and income on the assumption that there is no borrowing or lending.

If all payments and receipts were anticipated with absolute certainty, then the amount of money which would be demanded for transactions purposes would equal the active money requirement of the system. This is not, of course, true of the real world and we must consider the effect of uncertainty as to future transactions.

It is in connection with this uncertainty that the first element in the Keynesian precautionary demand comes in. We recall the wording: 'for contingencies requiring sudden expenditure and for unforeseen opportunities of advantageous purchase'. In other words, the future being uncertain there is a risk of being disadvantaged by not having surplus money available over and above that which is earmarked for known requirements. The marginal satisfaction from holding such balances will decrease with the amount held, other things being equal, and the demand will be income-elastic both because contingency provision tends to be related to the scale of operations and because of the falling marginal opportunity cost of holding money as income rises. We can summarize the factors examined so far by expressing the demand for money as a means of payment, $(L_1)$, in a situation in which there is no borrowing and lending, as two elements functionally related to money-income $(Y)$ thus

$$L_1 = f_i(Y) + f_p(Y).$$

[5] Ellis, H. S. (op. cit.) has given precise mathematical form to the degree of overlapping $(g)$ as follows:

$$g = \frac{vl - il}{vl - m}$$

where  $i$ = average income-expenditure period
       $v$ = average payments interval
     $m$ = maximum payments interval
      $l$ = number of stages (weighted by money flows).

where $f_t(Y)$ represents the transactions demand under perfect certainty and $f_p(Y)$ the additional precautionary demand.

## 2. Money as a Store of Value

We have examined the factors determining the demand for money as a means of payment, in the absence of financial transactions; we shall now (equally artificially) leave aside the means of payment aspect and consider money purely as a store of value.

As a first approach to this problem it will be necessary to examine in a very general way the factors underlying choice of assets. In this examination we shall be concerned with stocks of wealth as distinct from flows, and our object will be to explain, given the quantity of wealth which individuals or firms possess, the way in which they will distribute this wealth between various assets.

In a highly developed economy like that of the United Kingdom, with complex and highly specialized financial institutions and financial instruments, the choice open to individuals and firms with regard to the form in which wealth may be held is infinitely varied. They may, for example, choose between holding wealth in currency, demand deposits, time deposits, savings bonds, Treasury Bills, short-term government securities, long-term government securities, debentures, preference shares, ordinary shares, stocks of consumer goods, and productive equipment. Moreover, within many of these classes there are many sub-classes.

For our present purpose we must first distinguish between financial assets and real assets. Financial assets are essentially claims; real assets are either durable consumer goods from which utility is obtained directly, or durable factors of production which, when combined with current factors of production, produce goods from which utility is obtained directly. The choice between real and financial assets is different in character from that between different classes of financial assets, because the return on the latter is obtainable by passive ownership, while, in general, the return on the former requires entrepreneurship. We therefore leave this choice for consideration in connexion with the determination of investment and concentrate on the choice between financial assets. Within these financial assets we must include claims representing real capital, since they reflect institutional arrangements which permit entrepreneurship and ownership to be divorced.

The general principle of portfolio selection is easily stated: it is that funds which it is not intended to spend on real goods either for consumption or investment will be held in such proportions of the available financial assets as will make their marginal yields equal. This principle underlies all our analysis of financial asset choice, but we need to go beyond this and consider the particular characteristic of each of the main types of financial assets in order to show the relative advantages and disadvantages upon which this marginal valuation is based. Observed relative yields are our only empirical data—for the rest we must rely upon *a priori* reasoning.

We shall therefore consider the three main types of financial asset: money, bonds, and equities, and we shall consider the characteristics of these assets (other than their yield) under five heads:

A. Cost
B. Marketability
C. Money-value certainty
D. Income certainty
E. Real-value certainty

### A. Cost

The first element included under this head is the cost, if any, of the transaction which is involved in acquiring the asset. For example, the purchase of any kind of security involves the purchaser in brokerage and some involve stamp duty. In addition to the money cost of buying the asset, we must also represent the inconvenience of the transaction as having some cost.

### B. Marketability

By marketability we mean the extent to which there is a ready market for the asset. Clearly, in a money economy, except in exceptional circumstances, an asset can always be disposed of at some price. The extent to which a capital loss has to be faced in order to dispose of an asset falls for consideration under the next of our headings; here we are concerned simply with the breadth and efficiency of the market for the particular asset. In general it may be said that the less specific is the asset the greater will be its marketability.

## C. Money-Value Certainty

This would be said to be present if there were no risk of fluctuation in the capital value of the asset in money terms. There is no asset of which this is absolutely true save money itself and those assets (*quasi-money*) which are identical with bank deposits from the asset point of view. With all other assets, since they must be sold at the current price in order to convert them into general purchasing power, there must necessarily be some risk of depreciation in money value. This also means that there is a possibility of money-value appreciation, and we have to determine what is the net effect on the mind of the investor of the risk of depreciation and possibility of appreciation.

This problem can be resolved, without making any introspective generalizations regarding the propensity of the individual to gamble, by employing a concept which is familiar in other fields of economics, namely the diminishing marginal utility of money. If the individual concerned suffers capital depreciation he will lose what we may loosely describe as 'intramarginal' units of wealth; if on the other hand he enjoys capital appreciation he will gain 'extra-marginal' units of wealth; it follows from the principle of diminishing marginal utility of money that the satisfaction lost by depreciation will be greater than that gained by an equal appreciation. Thus an individual will require some inducement before he will subject himself to this risk if depreciation and appreciation are equally probable in his mind.

## D. Income Certainty

We are not here considering the risk that the obligations of the contract will not be carried out, since we take that into consideration in the money yield. Under this heading we distinguish between two different types of contract: a legal entitlement to interest (a bond), and a share in the profits of an enterprise (an equity). Other things being equal, a bond will possess greater money-income certainty than an equity because of its prior claim on gross profits.

## E. Real-value Certainty

This is a characteristic which is dependent upon what is happening to the value of money. If money had a completely fixed and constant value in terms of goods and services in general it would have complete real-value certainty. But the value of money in terms of goods and services in general is not fixed and constant, and, by virtue of their fluctuating real value, money and bonds must be considered as inferior to equities which represent real capital. But though this is true of equities in general it is not necessarily true of particular examples, and the disadvantages of money and bonds under this head can only be avoided by running the risks of unprofitability associated with a specific form of capital. This risk is much reduced by investing indirectly via unit trusts.

We can now summarize the relative merits of the three categories of assets by allocating 'marks' to them with respect to the factors distinguished above. This is done in Table 2, in which all the symbols stand for positive values.

TABLE 2

*Relative Merits of Assets*

| | Cost | Marketability | Money-value Certainty | Income Certainty | Real-value Certainty |
|---|---|---|---|---|---|
| Money | $A$ | $B$ | $C$ | $D$ | $E-e$ |
| Bonds | $A-a$ | $B-b$ | $C-c$ | $D$ | $E-e$ |
| Equities | $A-a$ | $B-b$ | $C-c$ | $D-d$ | $E-e'$ |

Under heads $A$ to $D$ money scores full marks. It involves no cost; it does not need to be marketed to convert it into means of payment; it clearly has absolute money value certainty; its zero yield is also absolutely certain. It could only score full marks under factor $E$ if the value of money in terms of real goods were absolutely constant and it is therefore inferior to equities to an extent $e$, representing the uncertain future real value of money.

As compared with money, bonds are inferior under heads $A$, $B$ and $C$. They involve costs to acquire; their encashment involves market limitations which do not attach to money and they are subject to fluctuations as to their money value. Under heads $D$ and $E$ there is nothing to choose between money and bonds; the yield offered by both is certain and in both cases the real value is subject to fluctuations in the real value of money.

Equities are similarly inferior to money under heads $A$, $B$ and $C$, and are also inferior to bonds and money under head $D$ because of the risks of the venture. It is only under head $E$, in certain circumstances, that equities can be superior to money and bonds, namely if the real value of uncertainty of bonds and money (represented in the table by $e$) is greater than the specific risk attaching to equities (represented by $e'$).

These relative marks have been assigned to the assets under the respective headings in the table in such a way that it is not possible to add them up for each asset. This has been done because we cannot assign cardinal values to these degrees of preference since we have no *a priori* means of judging the relative importance of the five factors.

Nevertheless, in the absence of knowledge of the relative weights, we can come to some limited conclusions. Considering only money and bonds, we can say that money will always be preferred to bonds unless there is some positive inducement to invest in bonds. The existence of such a preference is a sufficient condition for the existence of an inducement to overcome the unwillingness of people to acquire the inferior asset; the rate of interest payable on bonds is such an inducement.

If we consider the choice between bonds and equities, but exclude the factor of real value certainty, we can say that since equities are no more attractive under heads $A$, $B$ and $C$ but inferior under $D$ a further inducement, over and above that which is required to induce the holding of bonds, will be required in the case of equities. The greater yield which is normally obtainable from equities over that which is obtainable from interest on bonds is such an inducement. In this context the yield on equities must be taken to include such growth in capital value as is the result of ploughing back profits, which must be sharply distinguished from increases in real asset prices in general resulting from decreases in the value of money.

If we now introduce the factor of real value certainty we can go further and say that the fact that equity yields are normally greater than interest yields demonstrates that normally money income certainty is rated higher than real value certainty. That is to say, the disadvantage of an uncertain income from equities combined with their specific risk normally outweighs the disadvantage of the uncertain real value of bonds ($d + e'$ exceeds $e$) and the higher return is required to redress the balance. When, as sometimes happens, this normal relationship between interest on bonds and yield on equities is reversed it is evidence of a desire to 'hedge' against inflation; in other words the value put upon $e$ increases so that it exceeds $d + e'$.

In this section we are particularly concerned with the demand for money. The foregoing analysis has shown, in particular, why money should be held as an asset, in spite of the fact that it yields no financial return, in preference to income yielding financial assets. This preference is based on the second element in Keynes's precautionary motive namely 'to hold an asset the value of which is fixed in terms of money'. Here again, as in the first element in the precautionary motive, it is uncertainty which is the basis of the precaution. But it is a different object to which the uncertainty applies. In the first element it is precaution against uncertain payments requirements; in the second element it is precaution against uncertain capital values of all other financial assets. In order to carry further the analysis of the demand for money as a store of value it will be convenient to concentrate on the choice between money and bonds. We shall therefore assume that the relation between the yield on bonds and that on equities remains constant. This being so, bonds can be regarded as standing for all non-money assets. Moreover, we propose, in this and the following section to confine ourselves to only one type of security—a long-term bond on which there is no risk of default. Risk of default can always be superimposed on the analysis at any stage by simply adding a risk premium to the yield required by the lender. The complications involved in the existence of bonds of different lengths of life is not so simple, and we shall defer it until Chapter VI. For the time being our assumption of only one type of bond allows us to speak of 'the' rate of interest.

In using this abstraction, however, it is necessary to introduce a complication which is significant in empirical analysis, namely that interest is normally subject to tax. Indeed this applies to the money income received from the ownership of any asset, and the foregoing general statement regarding asset choice must be qualified, in that it is the net yield after taxation which should be taken into consideration in judging the relative attractions of different assets. We can, however, omit this complication from our theoretical analysis without altering any of the conclusions.

We can now establish a relationship between the demand for money as an asset and the rate of interest, on the above assump-

tions. The factors which our summary table shows to be significant to the choice between money and bonds are the costs of
investment and the uncertainty as to the money value of bonds.
Uncertainty as to the money value of bonds presents the investor with the prospect of capital loss or capital gain, but we have
argued that when these events are equi-probable the prospect of
loss will weigh more than the prospect of gain. We shall first
consider that element in demand which is present where expectations regarding future bond prices are neutral, that is to say
where appreciation and depreciation are regarded by the investor as equi-probable events. In this situation a positive yield
will be required to induce investment in bonds, and the greater
this inducement is the more of his funds will such an investor be
willing to invest in bonds. Hence the individual demand schedule will be negatively related to the rate of interest. Any fixed
cost of investment will have the same effect.

For one special class of people this relationship must necessarily be unvarying. Those who are in a position to hold bonds
indefinitely will have a zero demand for money as an asset at
any positive rate of interest, because the receipt of any return in
perpetuity must outweigh the fixed cost of investment, and the
question of capital loss on encashment does not arise. Since the
demand for money by this special class is always zero, it will
make no difference to our examination of the relationship
between the demand for money and the rate of interest if we
exclude all perpetual holders of bonds. For the whole of the
community the demand schedule must clearly be such that the
desire to hold wealth in the form of money increases as the rate
of interest falls. Moreover there must be some rate (the interest
floor) below which all investors (excluding perpetual holders)
will prefer to hold money. The demand schedule representing
this element in the situation is shown in Figure III.3 by the
curve $L_r$. Since it derives its shape mainly from the pure risk
factor (expectations neutral), we shall refer to it as the risk-
induced element in demand and write the function:

$$L_r = f_r(R, u)$$

where $R$ is the current rate of interest and $u$ is the degree of
uncertainty attaching to the money value of bonds.

If this were the only element in the demand for money it

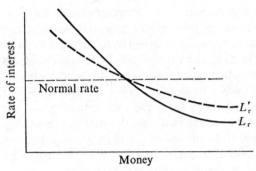

FIG. III.3. Risk-Induced Demand

would imply very simple-minded investors indeed, for it would imply that investors assign the same risk factor to the money value of bonds at all rates of interest, the variation in demand with changes in the rate of interest being due solely to different individual assessments of that risk. We must now go on to superimpose on this pure risk element that which is due to expectations which are not neutral.

One factor influencing expectations of changes in bond prices will be the relationship between the current rate of interest and normal rate. We visualize investors as deriving from past events some notion of the range within which the rate of interest is likely to move. We shall call this the normal range and the rate at the mid-point of this range the *normal rate*. Were this the only factor entering into expectations, the effect of superimposing it on the risk-induced demand curve would simply be to make the demand more elastic and to raise the floor, as shown in the curve $L_r$ in Figure III.3. This follows because the higher the rate of interest the greater would be the expectation of a fall in the rate of interest (rise in bond prices), and the lower the rate of interest the greater would be the expectation of a rise in the rate (fall in bond prices). In terms of pure risk this would tend to decrease the risk premium required at above-normal rates of interest and increase it at rates of interest below the normal rate. The effect of this would be to flatten out the curve above and below the normal rate as indicated in $L_r'$.

Everything discussed so far has depended on risk. In so far as expectations have been introduced they have been assumed to depend upon the concept of a normal rate. To the extent that all expectations were the same in the market regarding the normal rate, expectations would have a stabilizing effect tending to maintain the normal rate but expectations do not operate like that in the real world.

Normality is not the only concept which enters into expectations; if it were, there would be little opportunity to 'profit from knowing better than the market what the future will bring forth'. We have arrived at the third of Keynes's motives—the speculative motive.

The gain obtainable from a speculative purchase of bonds is obvious enough not to require any demonstration, but it will be well to make specific the gain obtainable from a speculative sale of bonds. If a bond with a nominal value of £100 which carries interest of £5 per annum stands at its par value in the market, then its current yield is 5 per cent per annum. If it is expected that the bond will fall in value so that it could be bought a year hence for £90, and the cost of selling and buying is £2, then a profit can be made by selling the bond now and buying it back again a year hence. If this is done and the expectation proves correct there will be a capital gain of £8 to set against the loss of £5 interest. Thus a net profit of £3 can be obtained by holding money instead of the bond for the period in question. Clearly the essence of speculative demand for money is the existence in someone's mind of a difference between current bond prices (rate of interest) and expected bond prices (rate of interest).

Our treatment of speculative demand must allow for expectations which are obtained by an assessment of the appropriate rate in particular circumstances, whether or not this is the normal rate. This means that in general expectations are likely to be dispersed about the current rate; some investors (bears) expecting rates to rise and others (bulls) expecting rates to fall. This *expectations complex* can be represented in terms of the net volume of funds associated respectively with bull and bear expectations as functions of the current rate.

There is a rate of interest, or range of rates as shown in Figure III.4, at which there is no tendency for the rate of interest to change as a result of expectations of a change in the rate of interest. This situation may occur either because everyone expects the rate of interest to remain unchanged or because there are two views in the market which balance one another. At this rate, or within this range of rates, net speculative demand for money will be zero since the expectations complex is neutral.

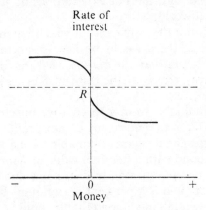

FIG. III.4. Speculative Demand

At rates of interest below the neutral position, expectations will be bearish and the speculative demand for money will be positive—increasing as the rate falls. Similarly, at rates of interest above the neutral position the speculative demand for money will be negative—increasingly so as the rate rises. Moreover the elasticity of demand will become infinite in both the positive and negative phases. In general we can express the speculative element in the demand for money thus:

$$L_s = f_s(R, R_x)$$

where $R_x$ stands for the expectations complex.

This presentation of speculative demand as having a negative phase differs from the generally accepted presentation as a result of the present treatment of speculative demand as separate from the risk-induced element. Negative speculative demand signifies a 'short' position in that component of money holdings and therefore implies that money held for non-speculative reasons is reduced below its normal level. That is to say, a positive expectation of a fall in the rate of interest (appreciation of bonds) will offset the risk-induced element and hence reduce the total demand. Similarly, a positive expectation of a rise in interest rate (depreciation of bonds) will be superimposed on the risk-induced element and increase the total demand.

The level of the speculative demand curve will be determined by the rate at which expectations are neutral, while its elasticity will depend upon the dispersion. In general the smaller the dispersion the greater the elasticity. In the special case in which expectations are completely concentrated the elasticity would be infinite and the demand for money function would be a horizontal straight line on the diagram which would imply that the rate of interest could not move; we shall refer to this situation as *speculative fixation*. Its essential characteristic is that there is a sufficient body of speculators prepared to release securities and absorb money whenever there is a tendency for the rate to fall, and to release money and absorb securities whenever there is a tendency for the rate to rise. In line with the general explanation of the significance of negative demand, we must regard the money released in the latter circumstance as being drawn from risk-induced balances.

In this connection it must be stressed that the level at which speculative fixation may occur is completely independent of the rate of interest floor which was derived from our consideration of risk. It is frequently stated or implied that the demand for money can only become infinitely elastic at some abnormally low level of the rate of interest.[6] This error results from a failure to make the distinction between the demand for money which is based on the risk of capital value change and that based on a positive expectation. When this distinction is made it is clear that the demand for money can become infinitely elastic at any rate of interest if there is a consensus of opinion that the current rate is the 'right' rate in the given situation. This may equally well occur at an abnormally high rate as at an abnormally low rate. This situation, however, is likely to be confined to the very short-term unless it reflects real factors affecting the rate of interest. In the absence of such factors there is a strong tendency for expectations to be concentrated at the normal rate thus imparting considerable inelasticity to the overall demand for money function.

We can now summarize the general conclusion of this section

[6] Modigliani, F., 'Liquidity Preference and the Theory of Interest and Money', in *Readings in Monetary Theory*, London, 1944, pp. 198–9.

by stating that, on the assumptions made, the demand for money as a store of value can be regarded as the sum of the risk-induced element and the speculative element. These elements are each functions of the current rate of interest, the former depending on uncertainty and the latter on positive market expectations. For any combination of these factors the demand for money as a store of value can be regarded as the sum of two elements both of which are functions of the current rate, thus:

$$L_2 = f_r(R) + f_s(R).$$

The same conclusion can be drawn by the approach used by some writers in which the risk-induced and speculative elements in the demand for money as an asset are combined. This involves assuming that all investors have expectations which can be represented as a distribution of possible outcomes having more or less certainty and varying range. The limiting cases are absolute certainty about a given outcome and complete ignorance over a wide range. This author finds it more realistic to make a distinction between risk-induced activity based on 'fear' and speculative activity based on 'hope' than to include both under the speculative motive. This approach differs from that of Hicks in that he calls risk-induced demand 'speculative': Hicks says 'money may be held for the Speculative Motive, even though there is no expectation of a fall in the price of securities. It may simply be held because of risk aversion. Behaviour of this kind is speculative behaviour though it is not based on Hope but on Fear.' This blurs an important distinction implicitly made by Keynes.[7]

The varying uses of classification and nomenclature can be very confusing and are unimportant except as a means of clarifying the fundamental principles. The classification and nomenclature used in the foregoing analysis does clarify the principle and has the advantage of sticking closely to Keynes in an area in which he showed his outstanding ability to reduce complex problems to penetrating simplifications.

## 3. *The Total Demand for Money*

In the first section of this chapter we considered the demand for money as a means of payment, assuming there were no

[7] Hicks, J. R., *Critical Essays in Monetary Theory*, Oxford, 1967, pp. 46–9.

financial transactions (lending and borrowing), and derived the relationship for a given payments complex:

$$L_1 = f_i(T) + f_p(T).$$

In the second section we considered the demand for money as a store of value, assuming we could ignore the transactions requirements, and derived the relationship for a given normal rate and expectations complex:

$$L_2 = f_r(R) + f_s(R).$$

This procedure has been adopted to enable us to treat separately the means of payment and store of value aspects of the demand for money, and it is the purpose of the present section to show how these two aspects combine. If the two aspects were entirely independent we could simply add the components together to obtain the total demand for money and relate this to the total supply. But the two aspects are not independent; they overlap analytically, just as the two functions of money, as a means of payment and as a store of value, overlap.

Money which we have described as being held as a means of payment cannot be regarded as uniquely income-elastic because the holding of it over time is the result of asset choice. If money is held against a future transaction, this is not simply due to the expectation or possibility of its being required in the future, but also to the fact that the yield from investing it in the meantime does not compensate for the risk and cost of doing so.

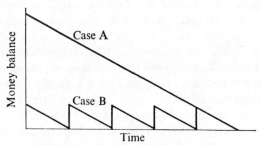

FIG. III.5. Economy of Active Money

If we introduce the possibility of lending and borrowing (which we excluded by assumption in Section 1), theoretically, the unique determination of the volume of money required to finance a given level of transactions virtually disappears. This can be illustrated very simply by reverting to the diagrammatic representation of the time shape of money balances which was employed in Section 1. Thus Figure III.5 represents the time shape of the money balance of an individual on highly simplified assumptions regarding receipts and payments. In Case A it is assumed that no lending or borrowing takes place; in Case B it is assumed that the rate of return on short-term investment is sufficiently high to induce the individual to lend part of his income on receipt and to recall the loan in instalments. In this way he is able to finance exactly the same pattern of expenditure as in Case A, the only difference being that, as a result of lending money which is unemployed within the payments interval, he reduces his income-expenditure period and thus reduces the monetary requirement of the system. This argument applies *a fortiori* to the precautionary element.

The extent to which an individual or firm will invest balances which are not immediately required as a means of payment will depend upon the relationship of yield to cost and risk for the period until they are so required. That is to say, it is a question of asset choice. On logical grounds, therefore, we must attempt to state the principles determining demand so as to cover both the means of payment and the asset aspects.

In practice this integrated approach is unnecessary in respect of a large volume of money holdings, either because the two aspects do not overlap in the case of certain classes of decision-units, or because the facilities for lending for short periods are either not available or the costs of doing so are prohibitive.

For most small-income-earning households the demand for money is uniquely determined by the factors considered under the transactions motive, and asset choice simply does not enter into the picture at all. At the other extreme there are financial institutions for whom there is no transactions motive and their demand for money is exclusively determined by the precautionary and speculative motives which we considered in connection with the asset function of money. For these groups the separate analysis already given is satisfactory, and the demands are additive. But there remains a significant group concerned with both aspects, and it is within this group that the volatile elements in decisions relating to monetary behaviour are located.

We turn, therefore, to consider a representative unit within this group of *transactor-investor-speculators*—a producing firm which is large enough to have a close contact with the capital market and sufficient funds to enable it to use available facilities at negligible cost per unit. Such a firm will have a 'financial policy' which can be separated analytically from other aspects of management. Let us assume that this policy is vested in a finance-manager and that he is responsible to the production department and to the development department for managing the firm's financial assets so as to maximize the return subject to the constraints imposed by the requirements of these two departments.

The production department will be regularly making payments weekly to wage earners, monthly to staff, quarterly to suppliers and (say) annually to the rent and tax collectors. Some of these commitments are so short term that even if the cost of investment in bonds were zero the risk premium required for investment in bonds in the interval would be higher than the yield obtainable in the short period involved, even at high rates of interest. If the risk of capital loss were rated at (say) 5 per cent of the capital sum then a rate of interest of 10 per cent per annum would be required to break even on an investment for six months. All funds required before that would have to be held in money.

In the same way the development department would require money for making payments at various dates in the future, probably going further ahead than a year, for such purposes as payments against work completed on building a factory, replacement of old machinery, installation of additional equipment, perhaps even a take-over bid.

These requirements could be drawn up in a schedule by the finance manager according to the most likely date of each requirement, and this would give a cumulative total of funds required to be drawn on at stated periods from the present. Given his estimate of risk premium and the objective data of the return on bonds and cost of investing, he would be able to decide how much of his existing money holding could be invested and how much should be retained in money form. This exercise would be repeated daily or weekly and his incremental demand for money would be determined, being positive or negative as the situation required.[8] There is no payment interval constraint.

We must now generalize this. We may visualize any finance manager as having at any time a stock of money and bonds which together constitute his total funds, to each unit of which he is able to assign a date of use. In some cases these dates will be absolutely certain, being determined by commitments into which he has already entered or by regular commitments the dates of which are known in advance; other dates will be less certain and will signify only that there is a possibility that certain quantities of money may be required at such and such a date in the future. These dates which he is able to assign to each unit of his funds determine the maximum period for which each unit of funds could be invested consistently with the transaction obligations; this we shall call the *encashment period*. Since uncertainty increases as we look farther forward into the future it is reasonable to suppose that there will be some finite limit to the length of the encashment period which any investor is willing to assume. That is to say he will act as if all of his funds were earmarked for use within some maximum encashment period.

Let us start by assuming no expectation of a change in the rate of interest and consider the choice between money and bonds on the basis of the break-even yield. This we define as the yield per cent per annum which is just sufficient to cover the costs and risk of investment in bonds. Since these are fixed costs relative to time, the yield required to cover them will vary in inverse proportion to the period of investment. This relationship is shown in the left-hand section of Figure III.6 in which the break-even function (a rectangular hyperbola) relates the break-even yield on the horizontal axis to the period of investment on the vertical axis. From this we can determine the *break-even period*, that is to say the minimum period for which funds must remain invested if the investor is to cover his estimate of risk and cost.

We now combine this with the encashment function $\varepsilon_1$ in the right-hand section of the same diagram. This shows the cumulative volume of funds (measured on the horizontal axis), the

[8] This approach is similar to the inventory approach discussed by Johnson, H. G., *Essays in Monetary Economics*, London, 1967, Ch. V.

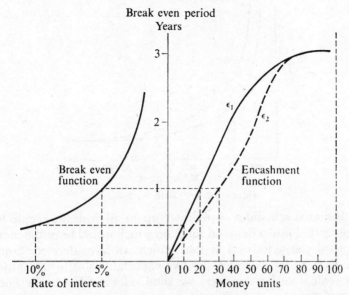

Fig. III.6. Break-Even Period

encashment of which will be required within the periods on the vertical axis. For simplicity the function is shown as linear over the significant range, and a maximum encashment period of three years is assumed.

These two functions together determine the demand for money in the absence of any expectation element. From the break-even function we can read off, for any current rate of interest, the break-even period; from the encashment function we can read off the volume of funds whose encashment period falls short of this break-even period: that is the volume of funds which will be held in the form of money. Thus at 5 per cent funds will only be invested in bonds if their encashment is not required for over one year. The encashment function shows that 20 units of funds are required within one year, so that 80 units out of the total of 100 will be invested in bonds and 20 units will be held in money. If the rate of interest rose to 10 per cent the demand for money would fall to 10 units as shown in the diagram. The demand for money derived from these functions is shown as a function of the current rate of interest in the curve marked $Y_1$ in Figure III.7.

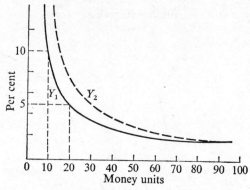

FIG. III.7. Non-Speculative Demand

If similar schedules were drawn up for all firms they could be aggregated into a demand function which would have the same general characteristics as that which we have derived. Since we have so far excluded positive expectations as to the future movement of bond prices, we shall refer to this as the non-speculative demand schedule.

We must now consider the effect of a change in the level of transactions, and this can conveniently be done in terms of the two functions employed above. With a given payments complex an increase in the total volume of transactions must mean a greater concentration of funds at the early encashment dates; such a shift in the encashment function is shown in Figure III.6 to represent an increase in the level of transactions which shifts $\varepsilon_1$ to $\varepsilon_2$. With the encashment at $\varepsilon_1$ and a current rate of interest of 5 per cent, the break-even period is one year; the volume of funds which can be invested for one year is 80 units, leaving a demand for 20 units of money. As a result of the shift in the encashment function to $\varepsilon_2$, the amount of funds which can be invested for one year is reduced to 70 units and the demand for money is increased to 30 units. The relationship between the two curves representing the non-speculative demand corresponding to these two income levels is shown in Figure III.7.

We have now to consider the effect of positive expectations. When we considered the speculative element solely with regard to the store of value aspect of the demand for money, we showed that dispersed expectations give rise to a function which becomes infinitely elastic in both the positive and negative phases (see Figure III.4). This must now be modified to take account of the limitation imposed on the finance manager by the encashment period.

This limitation depends upon the relationship between the encashment period and the interval which the speculator anticipates may occur before the expected appreciation in bond prices takes place. We shall refer to the latter as the *expectation period*. Only in exceptional circumstances will it be so short that it can be ignored. In general, funds can only be invested in bonds for a speculative profit if the bonds can be held until after the date by which the rise in prices is expected. That is to say speculative investment in bonds will be confined to funds whose encashment period exceeds the expectation period.

This means that some volume of funds (depending on the length of the expectation period) will be outside the influence of 'bull' speculation and will be held in the form of money unless the flat interest yield is sufficient to cover costs after the manner of non-speculative investment. For funds with an encashment period shorter than the expectation period, therefore, the demand will have the same characteristic as non-speculative demand.

This can be illustrated in terms of the encashment function $\varepsilon_1$ in Figure III.6 assuming a current rate of interest of 5 per cent. If it is expected that the price of bonds will have increased by 5 per cent six months hence, then ten units of money will be invested, in order to obtain the speculative profit, which would not have been invested in response to the incentive of the flat yield of 5 per cent. Thus the demand for money will fall from 20 units to 10 units. Why stop there? Why not invest it all? Because the expectation period exceeds the encashment period of these remaining units. In other words: because they will need to be encashed within six months they cannot be invested in bonds on the basis of an appreciation in value which may not have taken place until the end of that period.

Of course, individual expectations are not as precise as this in the real world, and this, together with the aggregation of individual expectations, smooths out the kinks which would result from such sharp articulation; the result is that the response of demand to speculative incentive is damped down in its negative phase for operators involved in transactions.

With this qualification the conclusion is that the general effect of speculation is to impart a highly unpredictable element into the demand for money as expectations of future movements of bond prices cause operators to go short or long on their normal money holdings in accordance with the speculative motive.

So far we have considered only bonds as an alternative to money. In a highly developed monetary system there is, as has been stated earlier, a great variety of financial assets all of which are substitutes for money *as an asset*, and some of which are very close substitutes. To the extent that such substitutes are available to an operator it is these in which he will invest short-term funds when the cost and risk of investing in bonds is greater than their yield.

This means that those who have access to such risk-free investing will take advantage of the small interest obtainable and reduce money balances to a lower level than that which they would choose to hold if bonds were the only alternative. The principle on which the demand for money is based is exactly the same however, as in the money/bond case, even in the limiting case where the demand is zero.

In highly developed financial centres such as the City of London the financial facilities are so efficient that a large commercial firm having access to them has no need of a money balance. Take, for example, the case of a large-scale merchanting firm disposing of a bulk cargo of grain purchased abroad. Having received the cheque at 2.45 p.m. a messenger will have deposited it at the merchant's bank at 2.50. The messenger then proceeds round the corner and at 2.55 deposits a cheque for the same amount drawn on his firm's bank account to one of the London discount houses. Moreover, he probably passes in his walk a messenger of the buying firm who has collected a cheque of similar amount from another discount house and deposited it in the buyer's bank at 2.45 p.m. Even if the messengers had gone the other way round the effect would have been the same at the clearing later that afternoon—zero bank balances for both firms in spite of very large transactions: the limiting case of zero demand resulting from the availability of near substitutes.

At the other extreme there are pure transactors to whom the analysis of Section 1 applies. Moreover, the majority of the money stock is administered by individuals for whom the question of lending and borrowing between payments intervals simply does not arise. Nor are they concerned with asset choice in a volatile way. Less than 35 per cent of total deposits is held by companies, public corporations, and government; the remaining 65 per cent is classified as 'other', which is predominantly individuals. Certainly the bulk of this large proportion of the money stock will be held by the less affluent and less sophisticated majority who have little opportunity to act as anything but transactors, except for regular saving through non-bank financial intermediaries.

It has been estimated that if transactions costs in terms of time and effort are calculated at \$2 per transaction no investment in a risk-free asset would be profitable out of a monthly salary of \$1,600 (1969 prices) at a rate of interest of 6 per cent.[9] Income elasticity of demand is thus unity and Case A in Figure III.5 applies.

In a 'portfolio' specification of the demand for money, capital wealth would normally appear as the constraint variable, and the combination of capital with income in this respect goes back to Marshall, who postulated that people would wish to hold a certain proportion of their property in money form *in addition to* a money balance bearing a certain proportion (Cambridge $K$) to their incomes.[10] Following Keynes this element will be disregarded until it is fully discussed in Chapter VII.

We conclude this section with a general statement summarizing the principles on which this presentation of the demand for money is based. Funds will be held in the form of money if the investor's estimate of the inconvenience, cost, and risk of investing in available alternative assets exceeds the yield (including any expected change in the capital value) to the date at which he anticipates the need for encashment, having regard to his future commitments both certain and uncertain.

For a given payments complex and expectations complex we can write the total demand for money thus:

$$L = \psi(R, Y).$$

[9] Orr, D., *Cash Management and the Demand for Money*, New York, 1970.
[10] Marshall, A., *Money Credit and Commerce*, London, 1923, bk. 1, p. 44.

The analysis of the demand for money in this chapter has been made on the implicit assumptions of (i) constant prices, (ii) a closed economy, and (iii) asset choice restricted to money and bonds. These simplifying assumptions will be removed in Chapters VI and VII.

# IV

## MONETARY CIRCULATION

So far we have been studying money primarily as a stock, and we now propose to turn to consider the flow aspect. The distinction between flow and stock concepts and their mutual relationship is of very great importance in monetary analysis, and it is worth considering it for a moment. We have been talking about the demand for money in the sense of demand to hold a certain money balance at a particular time. This demand is confronted with the actual stock of money existing at that time. A stock must have a specific *date* attached to it or it has no meaning. A flow of money, such as income, on the other hand, is a rate of flow per unit of time and it has to have a specific *period* attached to it (per month or per year) or it has no meaning.

The relationship between stocks of money and income flows is such that the behaviour of the system can be described in terms of either. A flow out of a stock is a rate of change of that stock; an increase in a flow is the same as an increase in the rate of turnover of the related stock. The relationships are exactly demonstrated in a hydraulic model and use will be made of this analogy later in this chapter.

It will be recalled that we started our analysis of the demand for money with a division of the money stock into active and idle money. This division was established on the basis of a formal definition of active money related to the income-expenditure period, assuming that no lending and borrowing takes place. To match this in flow terms we can distinguish between the *industrial circuit* and the *financial circuit*.[1] The former is composed of all points at which intermediate or final transactions in respect of current production take place; the latter comprises all points at which lending and borrowing, or the buying and selling of existing assets takes place. If in terms of the analysis of Chapter III, the economy were populated exclusively by transactors on the one hand and investor-speculators on the other,

[1] Keynes, J. M., *Treatise on Money*, London, 1930, pp. 47–8.

the former would handle the industrial circulation and the latter the financial circulation. The money in the industrial circuit would correspond with active money, and that in the financial circuit with idle money: 'idle' because it is not generating current income.

In order to develop the analysis in flow terms it is necessary to introduce the concept of the *velocity of circulation*[2] of money. This is an old-established central concept in monetary theory; it is, however, capable of meaning a number of different things which must be clearly distinguished. In very general terms it is easily comprehended; it is simply a measure of the speed of turnover of a particular stock of money. More precisely, it may be defined as the relation between a stock of money and the value of transactions performed with that money per unit period. In order that the precise meaning of the concept may be clearly indicated it is necessary that it should possess two complements, one to indicate what is included among the transactions and the other to indicate what is included in the money stock.

We will clarify first of all the distinction relating to transactions within an industrial circuit, namely that between the transactions velocity on the one hand and income velocity on the other. The difference is simply that between expressing the speed of money as the time taken in passing from stage to stage in an industrial circuit and expressing it in terms of the time taken in passing round an entire income generating circuit. Putting this in terms of our precise definition of velocity, we may say that in order to calculate the transactions velocity of a certain stock of money within any industrial circuit we should add together the value of transactions at all stages per unit period and divide this by the money involved. This would be a measure of the number of times the money passed from stage to stage on average per unit period. In this calculation, by including all transactions within the industrial circuit, we should have included not only the final value of all goods and services produced during the period (the gross national product) but the value of all intermediate industrial transactions as well.

The concept of the income velocity of money, on the other

[2] Holtrop, M. W., 'Theories of the Velocity of Circulation of Money', *Economic Journal*, History Supplement, 1929.

hand, is that of the number of times (on average) that the money completes the entire industrial circuit per unit period. In terms of our precise definition it is obtained by dividing the money stock into the value of the national product.

It will be clear that the relationship between the transactions velocity and the income velocity will depend upon the number of stages. Here again the number of stages must be interpreted as in Chapter III with reference to the volume of money passing through them. The relationship between the values of the two velocities is then as follows:

$$V = \frac{V_t}{n}$$

where $V$ is income velocity, $V_t$ is transactions velocity and $n$ is the number of stages as defined in Chapter III.

We have also distinguished the different versions of the velocity of circulation according to whether we are considering the total money stock or only some part of it. Thus the concept of the velocity of circulation has a very different meaning if we are speaking of the velocity of total money from that which it has if we are speaking of the velocity of money in the industrial circuit or the financial circuit separately.

Calculations of the volume of transactions relating to the different circulations were made for the United Kingdom in 1930 by Shackle and Phelps-Brown,[3] and have again been calculated on a comparable basis (including some slight adjustments to the 1930 figures) by Welham for 1950 and 1957.[4] The results are shown in Table 3.

## TABLE 3

### Monetary Circulation

| Transactions £1,000 m per year: | 1930 | 1950 | 1957 |
|---|---|---|---|
| Financial | 54·5 | 120·8 | 204·1 |
| Industrial | 18·6 | 54·8 | 84·9 |
| Income | 3·9 | 10·8 | 17·7 |
| Velocity of Total Money: | | | |
| Industrial Velocity | 7·34 | 6·72 | 9·45 |
| Income Velocity | 2·20 | 1·75 | 2·70 |

[3] Shackle, G. L. S., and Phelps-Brown, E. H., London and Cambridge Economic Service Special Memo., no. 46, 1938.

[4] Welham, J. P., 'A Study of the statistics of the Monetary Circulation of the United Kingdom', Ph.D. thesis, University of Leeds.

These figures show very clearly the dominance of the financial circulation, and the ratio between the industrial transactions and income transactions indicates an average of 3·5 stages in the production process and that this has remained fairly constant.

Calculation of the two circuit velocities is not possible since there is no way of knowing how much of the total money stock is involved in the financial and industrial circuits respectively. It is certain, however, that only a small part of the total stock of money is actually involved in financial transactions. Since the total volume of transactions is of the order of seventeen times that of income transactions in all three years there is ample evidence of very high financial velocity. This is not surprising when it is realized that the financial circulation includes the following types of transactions: commodity markets; existing assets; new issues; existing securities; foreign exchange; the money market (accounting for well over half total financial transactions); other borrowing and lending.

If we suppose for a moment that the amount of money in each circuit could be distinguished, then the income velocity of total money could be expressed as a weighted average of these two velocities. When we are using velocity in the income-generating sense it follows that the velocity of circulation of money in the financial circuit is zero. Circuit velocity of total money is therefore determined by two elements: (i) the distribution of money between the industrial and financial circuits, and (ii) the velocity in the industrial circuit. This relationship is expressed in the following equation:

$$V = \frac{V_1 \times M_1 + V_2 \times M_2}{M_1 + M_2}$$

where $V$ is the velocity of total money; $M_1$ is money in the industrial circuit and $V_1$ its velocity; $M_2$ is money in the financial circuit and $V_2$ its velocity.

Since $V_2$ is zero, $V_2 \times M_2$ is zero, and the equation becomes:

$$V = \frac{M_1}{M} \times V_1.$$

Alternatively we can obtain the same result by combining the two equations:

$$V = \frac{Y}{M} \quad \text{and} \quad M_1 \times V_1 = Y.$$

From this it follows that the level of transactions can increase, with a constant industrial velocity, if money which had previously been restricted to the financial circulation is 'activated' by being injected into the industrial circuit, thus raising the velocity of circulation of total money.

This way of expressing the matter is the equivalent in flow terms of our earlier stock analysis. There we arrived at a transaction money requirement expressed as a fraction of income; in flow terms the velocity of circulation of active money is simply the inverse of this fraction. But it has been shown that it is not possible to distinguish a separate transactions component of the money stock because money is constantly moving backwards and forwards between the industrial and financial circuits as a result of lending and borrowing. Just as this complication was embraced within the general principles covering the demand for money in our stock analysis, so it is embraced within the concept of the velocity of total money in the flow analysis. Useful as the concept of active velocity may be for purposes of exposition, it is the activity of the total money stock which is really significant for monetary analysis, and it is with this variable that we shall be concerned henceforward.

The use of this concept of velocity makes possible a distinction between the quantity of money and the volume of 'money use' which can be made clear by the use of the equation of exchange associated with the name of Irving Fisher.[5]

$$M \times V \equiv P \times T$$

where $M$ is total money, $V$ its velocity, $P$ the general level of prices and $T$ the volume of transactions. This equation is essentially a statement of identity since velocity is defined as $PT/M$.

Transactions can be taken to mean any of the three things which were considered above: all transactions performed by money; all industrial transactions (intermediate and final); or

[5] Fisher, I., *The Purchasing Power of Money*, New York, 1926.

only final income transactions. Which of these is taken will determine the meaning of velocity in the particular context and the nature of the related price level.

The most useful of the three is the version in which only final income transactions are considered, that is to say, for $P \times T$ we can alternatively write $Y$ representing the money value of income. This equation holds irrespective of whether the change in the money value of income represents change in real income or simply a change in prices. We thus have, as an identity:

$$M \times V \equiv Y \quad \text{and hence:} \quad M \equiv \frac{1}{V} Y.$$

This identity must be distinguished from the 'behaviour equation' which postulates that:

$$M = k(Y)$$

where $k$ (generally known as 'Cambridge $K$') is a constant. If this postulate were true, and output fixed, then velocity (the inverse of $k$) would be constant and the most extreme form of the *quantity theory of money* would hold: any change in $M$ would give rise to a proportional change in $Y$, and if output ($T$) is assumed to be fixed, this would mean a proportional change in the general level of prices ($P$).

The constant relation between the quantity of money and prices implicit in this crude quantity theory rests on the assumption that expenditure is regulated by the desire to hold total money balances equal to some proportion of income. The argument was as follows: if $M$ increased, money balances would rise above the desired proportion of income and thus cause increased expenditure; this would not, of course, reduce $M$ in aggregate, but, with $T$ fixed, would cause $P$ to rise until the desired ratio between $M$ and $Y$ (that is $P \times T$) was re-established. But it was never quite clear in this argument how $M$ increased. If money were to rain down from the clouds there would undoubtedly be some such wealth effect as this, though it would be much more complicated than in this simple quantity theory effect because people need not correct their money balance to the desired level by altering their expenditure on real goods; they can do so by buying or selling financial assets. Moreover additional money does not come into people's hands in this way and later it will be necessary to consider the wealth effects of changes in the quantity of money as one element only in the whole assets/liabilities complex of the public.

.In view of the magnitude of the money stock which is associated with income transactions, it would be surprising indeed if there were not, over long periods of time, a very close association between the stock of money and income if only because a large amount of money is linked by a technical coefficient to income in some fairly rigid proportion. But this does not mean that all the money stock is so involved, and we have seen that the overall relationship between the total stock of money and income is the result of the distribution of the flow of money between the two circuits, or (which is saying the same thing) between the active and idle components of the total stock of money.

Changes in this distribution reflect changes in the activity of money and show themselves in the statistics as changes in the numerical value of income-velocity of total money. But this only describes something which is happening to money as a result of economic decisions on the part of individuals who act for households, firms, financial institutions, and governments. It is necessary to go behind this observable monetary behaviour and explain the human decisions which give rise to this behaviour. For this purpose we shall use the simplest version of the Keynesian model of aggregate demand in order to examine how money works in the income generation process and how it affects that process. First of all, however, we must define our terms.

In national income accounting the three aggregates, output $(O)$, income $(Y)$ and expenditure $(E)$ are identities reflecting from three different aspects what is happening to real resources. Thus we have the following set of identities:

$$Y \equiv O \equiv E \equiv C + I \equiv C + S$$
$$S \equiv Y - C$$
$$I \equiv O - C$$
$$S \equiv I$$

These correctly reflect the fact that the real income of an economy is identical with its net current output and that what is not consumed out of net output must have been added to the stock of capital either in fixed capital formation or in additions to stocks. Thus savings is simply another word for investment which it is convenient to use when classifying according to the source. Similarly expenditure in national accounting terminology includes *imputed* expenditure on unsold stocks and is therefore identical with current output and is simply another term for output analysed according to its disposal.

The aggregates used in the monetary analysis in this book are, appropriately, actual money flows. It is clear that there is no reason to expect that the money flow of actual final expenditure on goods and services should always be flowing into the retail end of the production system at the same rate as current production is proceeding. Nor need it be the case that the owners of factors of production are receiving income at the same rate as either current output or current final expenditure. Accordingly there is no necessity for savings (current income minus current consumption) to equal current investment-expenditure. These flows will differ whenever money is being extracted from or injected into the income generating circuit because there are time lags between the different points in the circuit to which these aggregates refer.

To mark the difference between the concepts used in our monetary analysis and those used in national accounting we shall use the terms *voluntary-savings* and *investment-expenditure* and we shall prime the related symbols.

Using these money flow concepts we can now introduce our hydraulic analogy which is shown in the diagram on the next page (Figure IV.1).[6] This shows liquid representing money flowing through the industrial and financial circuits of a closed economy. We start with Income $(Y)$ being disposed of either on consumption $(C)$ or voluntary-savings $(S')$ after taxation $(T)$ has been deducted for the finance of government expenditure $(G)$.

The $S'$ flow goes automatically into the stock of idle money $(M_i)$ represented in the top tank. This reflects the situation we have already recognized that saving effected in the medium of exchange simply makes money idle. Idle money can, however,

---

[6] The flow diagram is based on the hydraulic model constructed in 1950 and used for many years at the University of Leeds for teaching. See 'The Phillips–Newlyn Hydraulic Model', *Yorkshire Bulletin of Economic and Social Research*, Vol 2, No. 2, 1950.

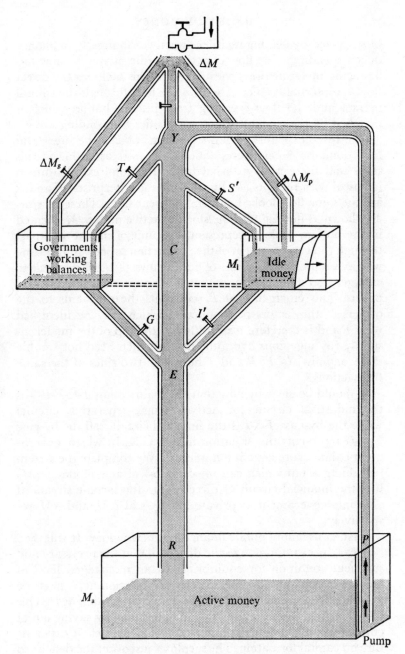

FIG. IV.1. Circular Flow of Money

be activated by lending it either directly or indirectly to finance deficit spending. The flow of activated idle money is shown as financing investment-expenditure $(I')$. This includes the direct flow via internal finance as well as the flow through the capital market and the flow resulting from intermediation which is matched by the issue of primary securities by spending units.

The three expenditure flows converge at $E$ to become total final domestic expenditure, and since we are assuming at this stage that there is no external trade, this total expenditure is identical with receipts $(R)$ by all domestic enterprises. $E$ and $R$ are the same flow looked at from different sides. These receipts are shown as flowing into the stock of active money $M_a$ located in the bottom tank. A representative unit of money will pass through the various stages of the production process in the same way as a representative unit of liquid flows through the tank to emerge, after a time lag, as payment of wages, rent, interest, and profits. This emergence at $P$ represents the payments to the owners of the factors of production which may be identified with $Y$ and is therefore transmitted to the top of the model instantly (by ingenious hydraulic means which need not trouble the economist) to $Y$; $P$ and $Y$ being the two sides of the same transactions.

It should be clear by now that the main circuit $Y$-$C$-$E$-$P$-$Y$ is the industrial circuit (or active income-generating circuit) while the by-pass $Y$-$S$-$I$ is the financial circuit and the by-pass $Y$-$T$-$G$ represents the situation in the U.K. in which government balances are kept at a minimum. We complete the system by adding a tap which can inject a flow of new money $(\Delta M)$ into the financial circuit or directly into the income stream at $Y$ or into government or private balances at $\Delta M_g$ and $\Delta M_p$ respectively.

First let us ignore public finance and new money. It will then be clear, by examination of the diagram, that the necessary and sufficient condition for equilibrium at an unchanged level of income is that the flow out of active circulation at $S'$ must be exactly offset by an equal flow into active circulation at $I'$. This would represent a situation in which all voluntary saving out of current income is being transferred to finance deficit expenditure on capital formation. The surpluses just offset the deficits so that there is no overall net deficit requiring new money, and total expenditure is equal to total income. *Say's Law*, which held that there must always be sufficient demand to purchase current output at unchanged prices, would be in operation. We can explain this, if we wish, by the hypothesis that $S'$ and $I'$ are kept in equilibrium by the rate of interest just as supply and demand of a commodity are kept in equilibrium by its market price.

But Say's Law clearly does not operate; and we first of all recognize that investment expenditure is the resultant of a complex set of factors among which expectations regarding future profitability is both dominant and highly volatile. We therefore visualize the $I'$ valve in our model as being under the control of company directors who make their decisions on investment expenditure on the basis of evidence outside the model. The savings valve is, however, automatically operated by changes in the level of income to reflect the basic Keynesian assumption that the marginal propensity to save is positive and less than one. The valve at $S'$ must therefore be visualized as opening as income rises and closing as income falls.

The reader will by now have seen that the model will perform the simple Keynesian 'multiplier' process for, us. We start from the state in which $I' = S'$ so that there is no change in the distribution of money between the financial and industrial circuits and therefore $E = Y$. It follows that $Y$ is not changing. We now increase $I'$ so that the flow through $P$ exceeds the flow at $Y$. With a time-lag depending on the average speed of turnover of $M_a$ (the circuit period of active money which is the inverse of $V_a$), this incremental flow will cause $Y$ to increase. This will cause $S'$ to increase by an amount determined by the marginal propensity to save.

So long as there is an excess of $I'$ over $S'$, $Y$ will continue to rise and with it $S'$. But this will decrease the excess of $I'$ over $S'$ so that the rate of increase in $Y$ will decline until it has become insignificant, with $I'$ again equal to $S'$, and $Y$ constant at a higher level. The increment in $Y$ will be determined by the leakage into idle money via $S'$ just as the increment in deposits was determined by the cash leak in the bank multiplier.

Thus
$$\Delta Y = \frac{\Delta I'}{1 - \dfrac{\Delta C}{\Delta Y}} = \frac{\Delta I'}{\chi}$$

In general:

$$\Upsilon_t = \Upsilon_{t-1} + I_t' - \chi(\Upsilon_t)$$
$$\Upsilon_t(1 + \chi) = \Upsilon_{t-1} + I_t'$$
$$\Upsilon_t = \frac{\Upsilon_{t-1} + I_t'}{1 + \chi}$$

Hence by iteration:

$$\Upsilon_t = \frac{I_t'}{(1 + \chi)} + \frac{I_{t-1}'}{(1 + \chi)^2} + \frac{I_{t-2}'}{(1 + \chi)^3} \cdots$$

Where $\chi$ is the marginal propensity to save, and $t$ stands for a period in time. This relationship can be expressed either in differential equations or difference equations: the adjustment process would give rise to a smooth curve in the latter case but the step-function of adjustment in successive periods is more familiar to economists. Both are shown in Figure IV.2.[7]

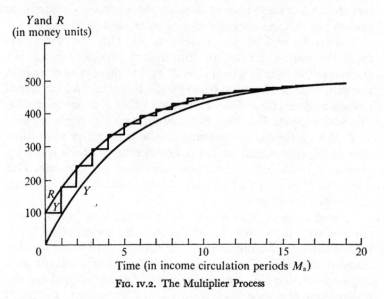

FIG. IV.2. The Multiplier Process

[7] The difference between the two curves is due to the attenuation factor being applied continuously in the one case and discontinuously in the other. The time-lag of $\Upsilon$ on $R$ in the step function is $\dfrac{1}{v_a}$ and in the continuous adjustment case it is

$$\frac{1}{v_a}\left(\frac{-\log_e(1 - \chi)}{\chi}\right).$$

The simple theory of the multiplier given above establishes a limit to the increase in income, but it says nothing about the interval which must elapse before this limit is reached. It will now be necessary to give some attention to the determination of what we will call the *multiplier period*. This we will define as the time which must elapse between an initial disturbance causing a difference between $S'$ and $I'$, and the establishment of the limiting value of income at which this difference is eliminated.

The multiplier process, if represented in difference equations, consists of a series of jumps in income which take place at discrete intervals equal to $n$. Since the amplitude of each jump is determined by $\chi'$ it follows that the time taken for income to approximate its limit must depend, given the value of $\chi'$, upon the length of the time-lag $n$.

It has been claimed or assumed by several writers[8] that this time-lag is equal to the circuit period of active money, but this is not correct.[9] The argument runs thus: the time-lag between expenditure and income is determined by the circuit velocity of active money, being equal to the average time taken for money to complete the circuit; a difference between $S'$ and $I'$ increases (or decreases) expenditure immediately; it follows that such an increase (or decrease) will be reflected in income after a period of time equal to the circuit period of active money.

This conclusion, though it seems highly plausible, is based upon a hidden assumption which is extremely unlikely to be realized in fact. This assumption is that individuals and firms throughout the industrial process always pass on any change in their receipts at the next payments opportunity. It thus denies the possibility that at any stage in the industrial process the producers may run down or increase stocks when confronted with a change in sales, and assumes that they must necessarily adjust production to an extent precisely corresponding with any change in sales. Similarly it excludes the possibility of producers, anywhere in the production process, increasing or decreasing production in response to a change in the level of sales at earlier

[8] e.g. Goodwin, R. M., 'Secular and Cyclical Aspects of the Multiplier and Accelerator', *Essays in Honour of Alvin Hansen*, New York, 1948, p. 108.

[9] Cf. Lundberg, E., *Studies in the Theory of Economic Expansion*, Stockholm Economic Studies, no. 6, London, 1937, p. 129; and Samuelson, P. A., 'Fiscal Policy and Income Determination', *Quarterly Journal of Economics*, August 1942; and Ackley, G., 'The Multiplier Time Period', *American Economic Review*, June 1951.

stages in the production process in anticipation of its impact on themselves.

The attempt to relate the time-lag between changes in expenditure and changes in income to the time taken on average for a unit of money to pass through the industrial circuit is logically invalid. This can most easily be demonstrated by means of a simple diagram. Figure IV.3(a) shows the behaviour of consumers' and producers' balances on highly simplified assumptions in which only producers and consumers participate in economic activity. It follows that any transactions which take place must move part of the existing money stock from consumers' balances to producers' balances or vice versa. It is further assumed that the payments interval is equal to one week and that the income-expenditure period is equal to half the payments interval. That is to say it is assumed that consumers pay out each week's income at a constant rate throughout that period.

For the first three weeks the diagram represents an unchanged level of income equal to one unit per week; the stock of active money is one unit which passes between producers and consumers once each week. At the beginning of each week the whole of this active money is in the hands of consumers; at the end of the period the whole of the money is in the hands of producers; at any intermediate point of time the active money is distributed between consumers and producers. The remainder of the money stock (idle money) is equal to five units, four of which are in the hands of consumers initially.

At the beginning of the fourth week an impulse is imparted to the system by an increase in the rate of expenditure by consumers; instead of spending one unit of money during the fourth week consumers spend two units of money. This reduces consumers' idle balances to three, and we have now to examine its effects upon producers. The assumption which is here made is that producers continue production at the same level and therefore make no additional payments to factors of production during the period. As a result producers' idle balances increase by one unit and this implies, of course, that producers' stocks of goods decrease by a similar amount.

This pattern is repeated in the diagram until period six, when producers, having decided that the new level of expenditure is likely to persist, revise their production plans and pay out to factors of production an amount equal to current sales. The result is that expenditure and income are now again equal and that the quantity of active money has been increased from one to two units. The remaining idle money has been redistributed so that consumers now hold only one unit and producers hold three.

The diagram then represents that in week twelve a further impulse is imparted by a reduction in consumers' expenditure which is treated in the same way as before by producers. The effect of this pattern of reactions upon expenditure and income is shown in Figure IV.3(b), from which it will be seen that the

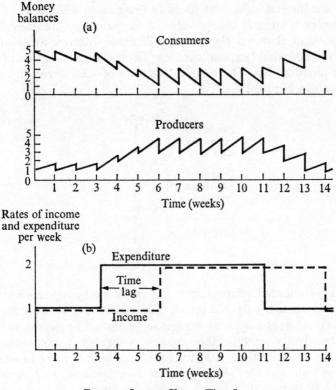

FIG. IV.3. Income-Change Time-Lag

time-lag between a change in expenditure and change in income is equal to three weeks. The diagram might equally well have been drawn assuming that producers delayed for any number of weeks before responding to the stimulus of increased expenditure. Indeed, if we permit the possibiity not only of delayed reaction, but of anticipation, it is no longer necessary to assume that the time-lag in which we are interested is a multiple of the income-expenditure period; it can take any value.

It will be apparent from the above argument that the period in which we are interested is not that which is required on average for a unit of money paid out as expenditure to move through the industrial circuit and reappear as income, but is the period required for individuals to respond to a change in the volume of money so moving. It is not the frequency of payments in which we are interested but the speed of reaction to amplitude. This time-lag is entirely independent of the payments complex and consists of elements classified by Professor Metzler as follows: (i) the household expenditure lag; (ii) the output lag; and (iii) the payment lag. The relative positions of these three lags are shown in Figure IV.4.

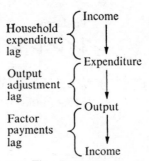

FIG. IV.4. Time-Lags in Income Circuit

The household expenditure lag is the delay in response by consumers to changes in income. The output lag is the delay in the response of output to changes in receipts. The payments lag is mainly the delay in the response of dividends to changes in profits. None of these has anything to do with the circuit velocity of active money, but statistical investigations by Metzler[10] have indicated that quantitatively the output lag is the most important, and it is in this position in the circuit that the lag is

[10] Metzler, L. A., 'Three lags in the Circular Flow of Income', *Essays in Honour of Alvin Hansen*, p. 11.

located in the above argument. Monetary theory, therefore, does not help us in determining the multiplier period—this is something which depends on individual reactions to changes in money receipts and may differ considerably in different circumstances. We are therefore left with a multiplier process which tends to an equilibrium without a date.

An important point to note about this equilibrium is that the process of establishing equality between the flows of voluntary-savings and investment-expenditure has resulted in a disequilibrium position with regard to stocks. This follows from the fact that expenditure exceeded payments to factors of production during the adjustment process. Since the total of payments to factors of production is identical with output this means a lag between expenditure and output, which implies a fall in stocks, the magnitude of which is equal to the increase in active money which is the sum of the diminishing differences between $R$ and $Y$ in Figure IV.2.

We could, of course, specify that investment-expenditure should include exactly sufficient expenditure on stocks by all producers throughout the system to maintain stocks at the desired level; rather than enter into detailed inventory-cycle analysis which lies outside our study, we simply note this possibility as an additional equilibrium requirement. We shall return to this possibility later when examining the condition for equilibrium growth. Meanwhile we note a tendency for changes in final demand to cause inventory disturbance.

Furthermore, in the simple exposition of the multiplier given above, we have made a very severe assumption, namely, that investment-expenditure remains unchanged in spite of the changing level of income. This is extremely unlikely, and the essence of aggregate demand theory consists in the interaction between the multiplier on the one hand, and the response of investment-expenditure to income changes on the other.

One way of representing this interaction is to make investment-expenditure depend upon the level of output,[11] so that where changes in money income reflect changes in output the response of investment-expenditure to income will be in the same direction as that of voluntary-savings to income.

Where this type of relation holds, the final increase in income

[11] e.g. Kaldor, N., 'A Model of the Trade Cycle', *Economic Journal*, March 1940.

depends not on the marginal propensity to save alone, but on the difference between this and the marginal propensity to invest. This follows from the fact that it is the difference between voluntary-savings and investment-expenditure which causes the change in income, and it is therefore the difference between these two variables which we must watch to see how it is affected by changes in income. If the marginal propensity to invest is less than the marginal propensity to save, the result will simply be an increased but still limited expansion. If the two marginal relations are equal, then income, once disturbed, will continue to change by a fixed amount per unit period for ever. If the marginal propensity to invest is greater than the marginal propensity to save, then the resulting income change will be explosive, income increasing or decreasing at an increasing rate per unit period.

Alternatively, it may be that it is the rate of change of income which determines the level of investment-expenditure, and we then have the *accelerator*.[12] Where this relation holds the results are more complex but still depend on the relative magnitude of the two relations governing investment-expenditure and voluntary-savings respectively.[13]

Finally we must complete the picture by showing the monetary and income effects of public-finance. The simplest demonstration is to increase $G$ in excess of $T$, and so long as we keep the absolute amount of tax-revenue constant the income effect will be exactly the same as that examined above in the case of an excess of $I'$ over $S'$. The equivalent multiplier base is now an excess of $G$ over $T$, but it is the propensity to save which determines the end result in which $S'$ will exceed $I'$ by the same amount as $G$ exceeds $T$. Alternatively, if $S'$ remains constant and $T$ rises as $Y$ rises (a reasonable assumption with most tax systems) the end result will show income in equilibrium after increasing by $\Delta G/t$ where $t$ is the marginal propensity to pay tax.

The more complex combinations of assumptions need not be elaborated here because our concern is with the monetary effects of a surplus or deficit on government account and par-

---

[12] e.g. Hicks, J. R., *A Contribution to the Theory of the Trade Cycle*, Oxford, 1950.

[13] Samuelson, P. A., 'Interactions between the Multiplier Analysis and the Principle of Acceleration', *Review of Economic Statistics*, May 1939, reprint in *Readings in Business Cycle Theory*, London, 1944.

ticularly with the way it is financed. To clarify this by means of the hydraulic model we make use of the connecting pipe which is shown with broken lines in Figure IV.1 between government balances and $M_i$. This connection precisely reflects the situation by which government borrows from the market such money as it does not cause the banking system to create through the tap $(\Delta M)$, and by which it maintains only minimum working balances.

The first significant point that must be made is that any means of financing a budget deficit will increase the financial claims of the private sector. This is equally true whether the money is borrowed from the market (drawn from $M_i$) or created on tap by the banking system. The difference between the two cases is that in the case of genuine borrowing the public get bonds while in the case of monetary creation they get money. If the budget deficit is financed by new money it is $M$ that increases, but if it is financed by selling bonds (or any other claim) to the public, then it is $V$ that increases.

This proposition has a more general application and is particularly important in respect of the distinction between credit created by the banking system and credit created by non-bank intermediaries. In general we can say that to the extent that $I'$ exceeds $S'$ there will be a reduction in $M_i$ unless this is offset by an equal increase in $M$. In the latter case the level of $M_i$ will remain unchanged. Credit creation to finance overall deficit expenditure $(I' - S')$ which takes the form of an increase in the lending of the banking system is identical with an increase in the money supply, so there is no fall in $M_i$. The increase in $M_a$ is offset by an equal increase in $M$ injected through $\Delta M$. If, however, the credit creation takes the form of increasing lending by non-bank financial intermediaries there will be no increase in the supply of money; there will be a fall in $M_i$ and an increase in the income velocity of the unchanged total money stock.

The direct effect on aggregate demand will be identical in the two cases. This is clear from the model because both are represented in the same way, namely by an excess of $I'$ over $S'$. In order to show how the monetary effects differ and, more generally, how money in its own right affects the decisions in the model, we have to combine our flow analysis with our stock analysis of earlier chapters and bring the rate of interest into the centre of the picture.

# V

## STOCKS AND FLOWS AND THE RATE OF INTEREST

THE intention in this chapter is to integrate the money stock demand and supply analysis with the flow analysis of saving and investment. This will be done within a simplified *IS/LM* model in which three assumptions will be made. These are: (i) constant prices, (ii) a closed economy, and (iii) asset choice restricted to money and bonds. These simplifying assumptions will be removed in subsequent chapters. Central to this model of aggregate demand determination is the rate of interest and it is useful in expounding the model to give some attention to the way in which interest theory has developed.

It will be convenient therefore to contrast four versions of the theory of the rate of interest: the so-called *classical* version;[1] the *loanable funds* version;[2] the *crude Keynesian* version;[3] and the *neo-Keynesian* version.[4] These different versions were developed in the order given, except that the second and third overlapped to some extent in the inter-war period and, as will be shown, may both be regarded as approximations towards the modern theory of the rate of interest here described as neo-Keynesian.

The *investment demand function*, although elaborated in the course of time, is basically common to all of the above versions of interest rate theory. It will be convenient therefore to set this out first, and for this purpose we must start with the *raison d'etre* of interest—the productivity of capital.

It is the productivity of capital that constitutes the incentive to undertake investments and a necessary condition for firms

---

[1] On the difficulty of establishing a precise statement of the 'classical' theory see Keynes, *General Theory*, pp. 175–6 and Appendix to ch. 14.

[2] Ohlin, B., 'Some Notes on the Stockholm Theory of Savings and Investment', *Economic Journal*, June 1937, reprinted in *Readings in Business Cycle Theory*, London, 1944.

[3] Keynes, J. M., *General Theory* and 'Alternative Theories of the Rate of Interest', *Economic Journal*, June 1937.

[4] Hicks, J. R., 'Mr. Keynes and the Classics', *Econometrica*, 1937, p. 147 et. seq.

to add to their capital stock is that the expected return from the investment will exceed the cost of borrowing the funds (or the opportunity cost of own funds) which is given by the current rate of interest. Keynes defined the return on investment as the discount rate $(d)$ by which the future stream of net income receipts must be discounted to equate their present value to the costs of production of the capital $(K)$. This rate is the *marginal efficiency of capital* $(MEC)$ which must exceed the current interest rate $(i)$ for investment to be undertaken. An alternative approach to the same criterion is the comparison of the present value $(V)$ of the net income stream discounted by the current rate of interest $(i)$ with the cost of production of the capital. The necessary condition is then that the present value $V$ must exceed the cost of production of the capital $(K)$.

That these are simply different ways of doing the same thing is evident from the following expressions:

(i)  $MEC = d$   where

$$\frac{Y_1}{1 + d} + \frac{Y_2}{(1 + d)^2} + \frac{Y_3}{(1 + d)^3} \cdots + \frac{Y_n}{(1 + d)^n} = K$$

(ii)  Present value,

$$V = \frac{Y_1}{1 + i} + \frac{Y_2}{(1 + i)^2} + \frac{Y_3}{(1 + i)^3} \cdots + \frac{Y_n}{(1 + i)^n}$$

If $d$ exceeds $i$ this is the same as $V$ exceeding $K$, from either of which calculations we can conclude that net investment will take place until the excess of $MEC$ over $i$ (or $V$ over $K$) is eliminated by the adjustment of the capital stock to the point at which decreasing marginal productivity reduces the $MEC$ to equality with the rate of interest. This is shown in Figure V.1. The question now arises as to the rate at which this adjustment will take place, because it is this which determines the amount of expenditure per unit of time which we need to relate to the rate of saving per unit of time.

The link between the marginal efficiency of capital and the investment demand function has given rise both to confusion and genuine disagreement. The confusion consists in representing the negative relationship in Figure V.1 as if it specified the rate of investment as a function of the rate of interest. The

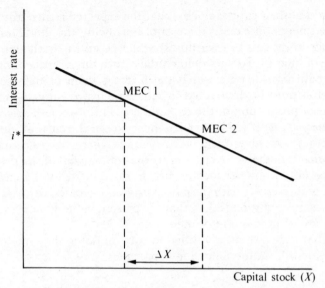

FIG. v.i.  Marginal Efficiency of Capital and Desired Capital Adjustment

decision to produce an increment in the capital stock does not, however, tell us the rate at which the capital stock will be adjusted. But, having made that distinction, there remains no general agreement on the rate of adjustment problem. One explanation is that of the rising cost of capital goods, but John Brothwell has pointed out that this formulation is not sufficiently general.[5] Given the normal assumption of constant costs up to capacity output it implies two extreme possibilities for the level of activity, one when the marginal value of capital is below normal supply price giving zero net investment, and the other at the point at which costs turn upwards as full employment is approached.

A more general approach to deriving a determinate rate of investment from the gap between the marginal value of capital and the price of capital goods is the argument that, at the micro level, the internal costs for the firm will rise as it increases the rate of capital formation in an attempt to minimize the time taken to adjust its growing capital stock to the desired size. This would give rise to a constrained rate of investment

[5] Brothwell, J., 'The Investment Demand Schedule and the Keynesian Equilibrium', *Yorkshire Bulletin of Economic and Social Research*, November 1968.

expenditure at the point at which rising internal costs have reduced the *MEC* to equality with the rate of interest. Since this is not a book on macro-economic theory and the model serves only as a frame within which monetary behaviour is examined, we will adopt this solution without going further into the issue.

On the basis of this relationship we can now deduce that the lower the rate of interest the greater will be the rate of invest-ment because it allows internal costs to rise higher consistently with profitability. The investment demand curve can therefore be drawn as in Figure V.2 as a negative function of the rate of interest and written thus:

$$I = \varphi(R).$$

In the classical version this investment demand function re-lating investment negatively with interest was combined with a savings function relating savings positively with interest which we shall write

$$S = \chi(R).$$

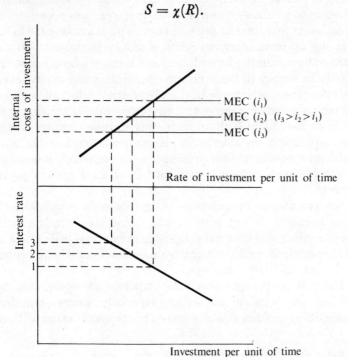

FIG. V.2. Investment Demand Curve

It was held that, in general, individuals have a 'defective tele-scopic vision of the future'.[6] That is to say, they normally prefer a given sum in the present to a similar sum in the future, the difference representing their degree of time preference. In order to overcome this difference in valuation the future repayment must necessarily exceed the sum presently sacrificed by a rate of interest.

In fact such a generalization regarding individuals' psycho-logical attitudes to the future as compared with the present is only relevant to the accumulation of personal savings, and even so it is both unwarranted and unnecessary. It applies only to the exchange of present consumption with future consumption out of the enhanced principal, and whether or not the rate of inter-est is required to induce such an exchange must depend on the income prospects of the individual. If we suppose that an indi-vidual has a constant income prospect, then the need for a pre-mium to induce an exchange of present consumption for future consumption follows from the basic economic postulate of diminishing marginal utility of money. This is because the saver is giving up intra-marginal units of money in order to obtain extra-marginal units; he will therefore require a larger number of units of money in the future to obtain the same utility, even with zero time preference in the above sense.[7] But an individ-ual with a decreasing income prospect may save at zero interest, while an individual with an increasing income prospect would pay a premium to anticipate his prospects, even if his time preference were zero. Our present concern, however, is how the choice between present and future is affected by *changes* in interest.

Modern theory recognizes two elements in the supply elastic-ity of personal savings with respect to interest—the 'classical' positive effect which we may regard as the normal price effect in market analysis, and the negative income effect which applies in the case of 'target' savings.

There is no presumption that corporate savings should be affected one way or the other, especially where imperfect competition enables firms to extract 'corporate savings' from

[6] Pigou, A. C., *The Economics of Welfare*, London, 1946, p. 25.
[7] Knight, F. H., *Risk, Uncertainty and Profit*, London, 1933, pp. 130–6.

consumers by raising the profit margin, or by appropriating resources by means of credit creation.

In the classical theory only the positive response of savings to interest was considered, and this, combined with the investment demand function, gave a traditional supply and demand presentation of interest rate determination as represented in Figure V.3.

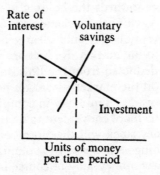

FIG. v.3. The Rate of Interest: the Classical Version

The important characteristics to note are that the classical theory is a purely flow theory and that the equilibrium between savings and investment is achieved exclusively by a rate of interest effect; these two characteristics will be compared later with those of the other versions.

By the first characteristic we mean that the variables determining the rate of interest are flow concepts as distinct from stock concepts; they can only be expressed as quantities per unit of time. In short, the equilibrium is that of a market which has to be cleared continuously, the flow on to the market being savings and the flow off the market being investment. The market is the capital market.

By the second characteristic we mean that if equilibrium between savings and investment were disturbed by a shift in one of the functions, then it would be re-established by a change in the rate of interest without any effect on, and without experiencing any effect from, any other variable.

The distinction of the loanable funds approach is that, starting from a more realistic understanding of the events of the capital market, its exponents perceived that the flow of money on to the market was not synonymous with voluntary-savings; nor was the flow of securities on to the market synonymous with the investment. More specifically, it was realized that the flow of money on to the market could be augmented or diminished by the activities of the monetary authorities, and that the flow of securities on to the market depended not only on the need to borrow for investment by issue of new securities, but on the disposition of investors towards the holding of existing securities. We will deal with each of these elements in turn.

Creations of new money should clearly be included in the flow of money on to the market. Reductions in the money supply can either be deducted from the flow on to the market or added to the flow off the market—it makes no difference to the results of the analysis. For simplicity in comparing the different approaches it will be more convenient to do the former, and the change in the money stock will therefore be incorporated into our analysis by adding *net new money* to voluntary-savings on the supply side. Net new money may of course be negative.

We pass now to the other correction which the loanable funds approach made to the classical equations. Although the relationship between the choice of assets and the rate of interest had to wait for fuller clarification by Keynes in the concept of liquidity preference, the loanable funds theorists had already perceived the importance of changes in asset preference in determining prices on the capital market. They saw clearly that, quite independently of voluntary-savings or investment-expenditure, a selling pressure could be produced in the capital market as a result of investors desiring to become more liquid. Similarly a buying pressure could develop as a result of investors parting with money balances in exchange for securities towards which they had become more favourably disposed as compared with money. Once these possibilities had been made explicit it was clearly necessary to incorporate them into any theory of the rate of interest. This the loanable funds theory did by its concept of *hoarding*.

Unfortunately, the term hoarding has become highly ambiguous[8] as a result of having been used in a number of different ways by different writers at different times, and even, in

[8] For a summary of alternative versions see Robinson, J., 'The Concept of Hoarding', *Economic Journal*, June 1938.

cases, in different ways by the same writer at the same time. It has been used in some places to mean a change in the holding of money and in some places to mean a change in the desire to hold money; moreover these two fundamentally different concepts have been variously applied to active money, idle money and total money respectively, and the same term used for all six versions. Not unnaturally confusion has abounded. It is no part of our present purpose to unravel these past confusions, but the reader who is perplexed by them in the literature will find that most of the difficulty will disappear if the word 'hoarding' is translated into the appropriate concept from among these six alternatives.

For the loanable funds theorists the appropriate concept was that of changes in the demand for idle money. They therefore corrected the classical equation by allowing for the fact that money might be demanded from the market in order to satisfy a change in dispositions towards assets, quite apart from the demand to finance investment-expenditure.

As in the case of changes in the supply of money, the arrangement of hoarding in the equation is simply a matter of convenience. Here hoarding is regarded as a demand for money; that is to say, a flow off the market; dishoarding, for the sake of symmetry, we shall add algebraically to hoarding, thus obtaining *net hoarding*.

Having made these corrections to the classical equations, we have, on the supply side, the sum of voluntary-savings and net new money, and on the demand side the sum of investment-expenditure and net hoarding; these constitute the supply of, and demand for, *loanable funds* respectively.

Diagrammatically the version of the determination of the rate of interest which is given above has been represented as shown in Figure V.4.[9] This shows the rate of interest determined by the intersection of the loanable funds supply and demand curves derived as above. It will be noted that the rate established differs from that which would be arrived at by the classical theory at the intersection of the savings and investment curves. Moreover, at the rate given by the loanable funds version there is a discrepancy between voluntary-savings and

[9] Lerner, A. P., 'Alternative Formulations of the Theory of Interest', *Economic Journal*, June 1937.

investment-expenditure. This discrepancy is equal to the algebraic sum of net new money and net hoarding. In market terms the demands on the market to finance investment-expenditure fall short of the current flow of voluntary-savings on to the market. This excess supply is being absorbed by the additions which the economy wishes to make to the stock of money held off the market.

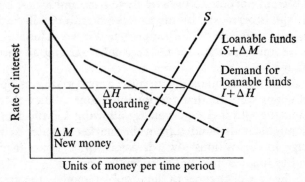

FIG. V.4. The Rate of Interest: the Loanable Funds Version

Let us now see what sort of a theory this is in respect of the two characteristics which we identified in the case of the classical theory: does the equilibrium between voluntary-savings and investment-expenditure depend entirely on a rate of interest effect? Is the theory a flow or a stock theory? Immediately we ask these questions we are in difficulties. In the first place there is no equilibrium between voluntary-savings and investment-expenditure; in the second place the theory is really a mixture of flows and stocks.

If we examine Figure V.4 critically the difficulties will emerge. It has been shown that the discrepancy between voluntary-savings and investment-expenditure is being absorbed by net hoarding; so far, so good. This conclusion is perfectly consistent with the modern version of the rate of interest theory, but if it is represented in diagrammatic form as a set of interrelated schedules there arises the difficulty of reconciling the flow and stock elements. The only way in which we can make sense of the diagram is by supposing a period too short to be of much value.

Voluntary-savings and investment-expenditure are straight-forward flow concepts, just as they were in the classical theory, but hoarding and new money are not. They are, in reality, changes in stocks, and as such they may reasonably be regarded as additions to, or deductions from, the market flows within the period during which the change is taking place. But a situation in which such change is taking place cannot be regarded as equilibrium, nor can a change in stocks from one level to a new desired level be commensurate with continuous flows. Volun-tary-savings and investment-expenditure are continuous flows which, at any given rate of interest, will continue throughout the Marshallian 'short-run period' at least. In actual time we may assume these rates of flow to persist over a year or more; it is otherwise with hoarding and new money.

It is one thing to say that during a very short interval market conditions will be affected by the creation of a certain additional sum of new money; it is clearly a very different thing to imply that at a certain rate of interest the monetary authorities will go on creating new money continuously at a constant rate through-out a period of years. This is the impression that is given by the diagram, because it implies that the flow of new money is com-mensurate with savings.

In the case of hoarding the reasons for objecting to the dia-gram are much stronger. Again it is reasonable to say that at some point of time, the rate of interest being at a certain level, people will wish to hold more money than they do, and to add the desired increase in money holdings to the investment-ex-penditure demands upon the market at that time. It is quite another thing to draw a schedule relating net hoarding to the rate of interest in the same way as is done in the case of savings and investment. If the statement of the diagram is translated into words it would appear to say that at a certain rate of inter-est people would wish to go on adding to their money holdings continuously at a constant rate over a number of years. This clearly does not make sense unless we bring in income growth as an argument.

In short, it is the schedules of net hoarding and new money that are wrong, because these changes in stocks are not func-tions of the rate of interest. If we confine ourselves to drawing the classical diagram and marking off some rate of interest other than the classical equilibrium rate, then the contribution of the loanable funds theorists is that of explaining how such a rate could exist in the market by reason of the effects of money creation and hoarding. The determination of the rate in the market in the Marshallian short period was not, in the loanable funds theory, capable of being expressed as an equilibrium of functionally interrelated variables; that integration is the particular characteristic of the modern theory of interest. It was achieved by virtue of the light which Keynes threw on the relationship between the desire to hold money and the rate of interest, but only after a deviation, which Keynes introduced, in the direction of a purely stock and income-effect theory.

We have called this the crude Keynesian version because it is that which is represented in the *General Theory* and in the immediately ensuing journal articles; in the later articles Keynes made certain concessions which modified the crude version sufficiently for others to put together the modern theory which we have called neo-Keynesian.

The crude Keynesian version is simply that the rate of interest is uniquely determined by the speculative demand for money and the amount of money available to satisfy that demand. The demand is given by the liquidity preference schedule $(L_2)$ and the amount of money available $(M_2)$ is total money less the quantity required to satisfy the transaction and precautionary demand. This is represented in Figure V.5.

It will be immediately clear that this version is a completely stock theory. Furthermore, whereas the classical theory attributed the equilibrium between savings and investment-expenditure entirely to the rate of interest, Keynes went to the opposite extreme and claimed that the determination of the rate of interest was nothing whatever to do with savings and

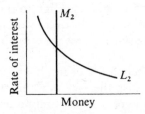

FIG. v.5. The Rate of Interest: the Keynesian Version

investment-expenditure.[10] The alternative equilibrating process which Keynes offered was, of course, the income multiplier based upon the propensity to consume. We have already shown in Chapter IV that on certain simplified assumptions any discrepancy between voluntary-savings and investment-expenditure will lead to income changes which will have the effect of restoring equilibrium. This was the major element in the revolutionary Keynesian theory of aggregate demand, and, as far as monetary theory was concerned, it offered a substitute for the classical interest-effect in the Keynesian income-effect; equilibrium between voluntary-savings and investment-expenditure in the Keynesian version being achieved entirely by changes in income.

This excursion into the history of monetary thought has been undertaken in order to contrast, with the necessary emphasis, the interest and income effects and the flow and stock elements respectively. It is the distinction of the modern theory, to which we must now turn, that it combines all four.

All of the elements of the theory have already been set out in more or less detail according to their monetary content in the foregoing pages; all that is now necessary is to collect them together and to work out their interrelationships. These elements have been expressed in the form of three equations as follows:

$$L = \psi(R, \Upsilon) \qquad \text{page } 61$$
$$S' = \chi(\Upsilon) \qquad \text{page } 85$$
$$I' = \varphi(R) \qquad \text{page } 85$$

We now add the equilibrium conditions:

$$S' = I'$$
$$M = L.$$

The most convenient way of representing the interrelationships implied in these equations is by combining them in a composite diagram. This is done in Figure V.6.

This diagram represents all of the elements in the above equations. Thus, Figure (a) represents the total demand for money as a function of the rate of interest and of the level of income; with a given quantity of money there is thus estab-

[10] Keynes, J. M., 'Alternative Formulations of the Theory of Interest', *Economic Journal*, June 1937.

lished a relationship between interest and income resulting from the satisfaction of equilibrium between the demand for and supply of money. This relationship is shown in Figure (b). Figure (c) represents the functional relationship between voluntary-savings on the one hand and the rate of interest and income on the other. Here again the satisfaction of equilibrium between voluntary-savings and investment-expenditure implies a relation between interest and income such as is shown in Figure (d).

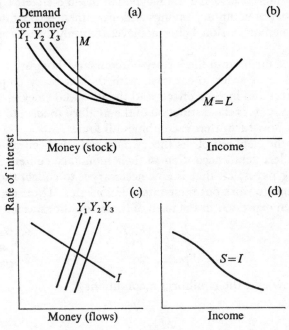

Fig. v.6. The Rate of Interest: Components of the Neo-Keynesian Version

It will be seen that the upper part of the figure exposes the indeterminate character of the crude Keynesian position; the rate of interest being left undetermined by the demand for and supply of money until the level of income is determined. Similarly the lower part of the figure demonstrates the indeterminate character of the classical position; the rate of interest being undetermined by the volume of voluntary-savings and investment-expenditure until the level of income is known.

In order to arrive at a determinate solution it is necessary to put these two versions together; thus, if Figures (b) and (d) are combined as in Figure V.7 the rate of interest and the level of income are mutually determined. This would have been described by Keynes in the *Treatise* as a situation in which the market rate of interest equalled the *natural rate*. In the *General Theory* however Keynes shows that there is a different natural rate for each level of income,[11] and the equilibrium income specified by this model has no tendency to establish itself at the full employment level; hence the need for government intervention.

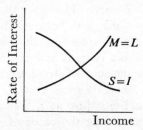

FIG. v.7. The Rate of Interest: the Neo-Keynesian Synthesis

Clearly this neo-Keynesian version is a combined stock and flow analysis, since it combines the stock equations of (a) with the flow equations of (c). We are no longer in the position of the loanable funds theorist, who simply made a qualification (though a perfectly valid one) to the classical flow theory on account of the effect of changes in stocks; nor are we in the crude Keynesian position of denying the effect of the flows on the stock position; we are at last in a position in which the rate of interest is seen to be determined both by stocks and flows and their mutual interaction. The fact that this analytical framework took so long to be accepted is surprising, not only because of its fundamental simplicity but because of its general application. The dependence of price on both stocks and flows is not something special to the theory of interest; it is applicable to any market in which there is a significant volume of speculation. Brokers operating on commodity markets such as the Liverpool cotton market or the London grain exchange use a combined stock and flow theory as naturally as the *bourgeois gentilhomme*

[11] Keynes, J. M., *General Theory*, p. 242.

used prose, and would no doubt be equally surprised to learn what they were doing. The market notes of such exchanges are full of discussion of the availability of stocks and the willingness to hold them on the one hand, the flow of production relative to the flow of consumption on the other, and the effect of these two elements on the market price.

To complete the modern theory we must take account of the subsequent recognition that it is not only new money (credit creation by the banking system) which has to be taken into account as a source of finance for deficit expenditure, but any kind of credit creation. This can be incorporated into the shape and slope of the $M = L$ curve. There are two possibilities here and it is important to distinguish between them.

With a given financial structure the non-bank financial intermediaries will have a normal pattern of behaviour which will be reflected in the velocity of circulation of a given quantity of money. In this respect Figure V.6(a) can be regarded as incorporating their activity just as it incorporates all other structural factors determining the value of velocity; similarly the diagram can be made to reflect the extent to which non-bank financial intermediaries are able to increase the velocity of circulation in the short-run in response to increasing demand for credit, by virtue of the loose linkage between their liabilities and reserves. This shows itself in a reduction in the extent to which the rate of interest rises as income increases. But, for the reason given in Chapter III, this elasticity of velocity must eventually tend towards zero, and the stable equilibrium character of the model therefore remains unchanged.

The necessary and sufficient conditions for this stability are:

1. that $MV$ is not infinitely elastic with respect to the rate of interest.
2. that $(S' - I')$ is positively elastic with respect to the rate of interest.

Assuming that these conditions are satisfied, let us examine the working of the model in order to see what part money plays in its own right as distinct from doing what it is told. In doing so it will be convenient to illustrate the verbal analysis by reference to the hydraulic diagram on page 71.

In order to reflect the propensity to save we visualize the

flow through the $S'$ valve as being controlled by the rate of flow of $Y$. For simplicity we assume that voluntary-savings is un-affected by changes in the rate of interest but incorporate an investment demand schedule by relating the flow at $I'$ to changes in the level of $M_i$. This reflects the assumption of a negative elasticity of investment-expenditure to the rate of interest which is measured inversely by the *level* of $M_i$. Thus if the level of $M_i$ falls as a result of an excess of investment-expenditure over voluntary-saving then the rate of interest rises. How much it rises for a given change in the volume of $M_i$ is determined by the slope of the end of the tank which reflects the liquidity preference schedule—an inverted version of the normal curve. This end of the tank can be adjustable to represent changes in liquidity preference, that is to say shifts in the schedule.

The interrelationship between the variables is best examined by supposing a shift in each of the functions in turn. Let us start with the marginal efficiency of capital. Starting from the position of equilibrium, we assume that for some reason business expectations improve and businessmen decide to invest more at current rates of interest. Diagrammatically, this is represented by opening the $I'$ valve so that a greater volume of investment-expenditure takes place. Since we started from a position of equilibrium, this must necessarily mean that the new level of $I'$ is in excess of the level of $S'$. As a result of this excess, income starts to rise in accordance with the normal multiplier theory, and since $S'$ is related to income by the propensity-to-save function, the volume of $S'$ also increases. This must cause an increase in $M_a$ and a fall in $M_i$, and the rate of interest must rise. But the investment function we have assumed implies that with an increase in the rate of interest the volume of $I'$ must fall. There are thus two factors at work tending to produce equilibrium between $S'$ and $I'$: on the one hand the increase in income is causing $S'$ to increase; on the other hand the rise in interest rates is causing $I'$ to diminish. The gap is thus being closed from two directions, not from one, as is assumed in the simple multiplier theory, and the additional factor is a purely monetary factor.

Equilibrium will be re-established when the gap has been completely closed, and when that occurs both $I'$ and $S'$ will be above their original equilibrium values, but below the level to which $I'$ rose as a result of the initial change in the marginal efficiency of investment. Similarly, both income and the rate of interest will be above their original values, but income will be below the value which would have been obtained had the full multiplier been operative. The actual values taken up by each of the variables will depend upon the shape of the functions, and the range of possibilities is limited by special cases which we shall have to examine. In general, equilibrium is achieved partly by changes in income and partly by changes in interest, and the final level of income depends not only on the propensity to save but also upon the magnitude of the interest effect. This in turn depends upon the elasticity of the liquidity preference function and on the interest elasticity of voluntary-savings and investment-expenditure. The greater the monetary effect, the more will the process of the multiplier be damped below its full value.

Let us now consider a shift in the voluntary-savings function. Let us suppose that for some reason, external to our model, the community saves more out of a given income. In the model this is represented by opening the $S'$ valve to give a higher level of savings at the existing level of income. Starting again from a position of equilibrium, this change must necessarily produce an excess of $S'$ over $I'$. Following the usual multiplier sequence, this causes a fall in income, as a result of which the volume of $S'$ diminishes. But with the lower level of transactions implied in the lower income there will be an increase in $M_i$. This will cause a fall in the rate of interest, which will diminish $S'$ and increase $I'$. Thus once again the gap between $S'$ and $I'$ is closed from both directions at the same time. Equilibrium will be produced when these two variables are equal, which will occur at some level intermediate between the original volume of savings and the level to which savings were increased as a result of the initial change. Here again the multiplier sequence has been damped by the interest effect.

Let us now assume an increase in the speculative demand for money, brought about by a change in expectations with regard to the future level of security prices. Diagrammatically, this is represented as a shift in the total demand for money schedule, so that at any rate of interest a larger quantity of money is demanded. In the model it is shown by an outward shift in the end of the tank increasing its capacity to hold $M_i$.

As a result of the increase in the demand for money the rate of interest must rise. With the rise in the rate of interest, $I'$ declines, producing an excess of $S'$ over $I'$. This sets off the multiplier sequence in contraction, and as income falls $S'$ diminishes. But at the same time the fall in income brings about a fall in the rate of interest, since there is a lower level of transactions to be financed. This fall in interest induces an increase in $I'$ and a fall in $S'$. Once again, therefore, the equilibrium is produced by a combination of income and interest effects, and the final position is one in which income stands at a higher level than would have been the case had there been no monetary effect. Thus once more the multiplier sequence has been damped.

Finally let us examine the effect of a change in the quantity of money. Starting once again from the position of equilibrium, the quantity of money is increased. This is represented in the model as an inflow from the tap into $M_i$ thus raising the volume of money available to be held as an asset and producing a fall in the rate of interest. At this lower level of interest, $I'$ rises above its original value and therefore exceeds $S'$. This starts off the multiplier sequence and, as income rises, so does $S'$. But with the greater volume of transactions there is an increase in $M_a$ and in the rate of interest, which cuts back $I$. This, combined with the income effect on $S'$, re-establishes equilibrium. The final value of income, voluntary-savings, and investment-expenditure is higher than it was originally but lower than would have been the case had the multiplier sequence not been damped by the monetary effect.

We can now generalize and say that the monetary effect consists in the imperfect elasticity of velocity with respect to income, which influences expenditure through the cost of borrowing to finance deficits; in the limiting case in which loans are simply not available the cost is infinite. The positive association between velocity and interest is illustrated in Figure V.8.

There are, however, certain special cases in which the monetary effect does not operate. The first of these is that in which the money supply is infinitely elastic to changes in P.T. From our analysis of the factors determining the supply of money we know that this means that the authorities are expanding or con-

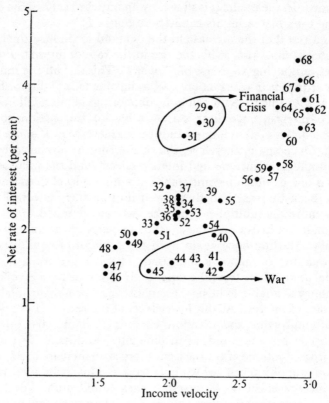

FIG. v.8. Circuit Velocity of Deposits and Net Yields on Consols

tracting the cash base so as to permit the money supply to expand or contract in response to changes in the demand for money. This is equivalent to a fixed rate of interest policy in which the monetary authorities make money available 'on tap' as the money market jargon puts it. Appropriately this is represented in the hydraulic model by manipulation of the additional money tap ($\Delta M$) so as to keep the level of $M_i$ constant whatever is happening to $S'$ and $I'$. The result is that the amount of money created (or destroyed) will be equal to the amount absorbed (or disgorged) by the active circulation.

$$M = M_a + M_i$$

and if $\Delta M_i = 0$ then $\Delta M_a = \Delta M$

With the supply of money thus infinitely elastic, the monetary factor as a positive element directly affecting expenditure disappears.

For the second special case we return to the assumption of a fixed money stock in order to examine under what conditions its velocity of circulation can vary so as to accommodate changes in the volume of transactions without the consequential changes in interest rates which the general analysis of monetary demand leads us to expect. One such situation we have already touched upon in Chapter V as speculative fixation. We saw there that, where there is a consensus of opinion in the market concerning the appropriate rate of interest, it is possible for the volume of transactions to change without any interest rate effect on investment-expenditure or voluntary-savings, the appropriate quantity of active money being released or absorbed by speculators. A similar situation exists at the interest rate floor. The common characteristic of these two situations is that the liquidity preference function is infinitely elastic. Both constitute a *liquidity trap* which renders changes in $M$ ineffective.

The third special case is that in which an expansion (or contraction) of expenditure is the complement of a voluntary decrease (increase) in the idle balances of the spender. Thus if a firm, for reasons such as we considered under the heading of asset choice, has been holding idle balances and then makes a decision to increase its rate of expenditure, the *voluntary* reduction in its own money balance will have no repercussion on the market for loans. The increase in the demand for money for transactions purposes is exactly offset by the decrease in the demand for money as an asset. In terms of the model the fall in the *volume* of $M_i$ is offset by a reduced capacity for holding it, represented by a shift inwards in the end of the tank leaving the *level* in the tank unchanged thus maintaining an unchanged rate of interest.

This special case is particularly important and is one of the main reasons for insisting on the unique character of money. Money is the only asset which can be drawn upon to finance expenditure without occasioning any monetary effect elsewhere in the system. To the extent that money balances held by potential spenders can be voluntarily released to finance their own increased expenditure there will be no monetary constraint on aggregate demand.

The simplified analysis given in this chapter is designed as a first step in the process of exploring the way in which money affects the real behaviour of the economy. In particular the hydraulic analogy incorporated into the flow diagram clarifies the relationship between the stock and flow aspects of monetary theory. At any moment of time the rate of interest must be such that the community is willing to hold the existing stock of money. Changes in the quantity of money or in liquidity preference can, in the short run, 'determine' the rate of interest; but it is also true that the rate of interest must tend towards the level at which the flows of savings and investment-expenditure are equal. The relationship between stock and flows will be a pervasive factor underlying the theory which is to be developed in subsequent chapters.

It would be possible to remove the simplifying assumptions adopted so far and deal with the modifications which must then be made within the $IS/LM$ frame. To do so, however, imposes some constraint on the analysis itself and some difficulty on the reader in understanding what is going on behind the posited shifts in the $IS$ and $LM$ curves. We propose not to confine ourselves in our subsequent analysis to elaborating a fully specified version of the $IS/LM$ model, but will use that analytical frame only when it seems appropriate.

# VI

# PRICE BEHAVIOUR AND THE OPEN
# ECONOMY

THE simple version of the *IS/LM* model expounded in the last
chapter abstracted from two questions which are both relevant
to the determination of aggregate demand and important in
their own right: price behaviour and the balance of payments.
We now turn to examine these questions, starting with money
and prices.

Starting at least as far back as Hume[1] there has been a
strong tradition in economic theory stating that in long-run
equilibrium the quantity of money affects the price level, but
nothing else. In its most rigid form the quantity theory of
money held that a given proportional increase in the quantity
of money would lead to the same proportional increase in the
price level. In terms of the Fisher equation $MV = PT$ introduced in Chapter IV, this assumed a constant velocity of
circulation and a constant level of transactions, which typically
followed from the assumption of full employment and a fixed
number of transactions per unit of income. This theory at once
provided the cause of inflation and its cure, whilst in its assumption of full employment, it assumed away the question of
money's effect on the level of real income and employment.

Two theoretical revolutions destroyed this position: the introduction of a behavioural approach to explanations of the
demand for money, which began before Keynes with Fisher and
the Cambridge school (Lavington and Pigou) but was later
extended by Hicks and Keynes; and Keynes's own demonstration in the *General Theory* of the possibility of involuntary
unemployment. For the relationship between money and
inflation hinges not only upon the relationship between money
and nominal aggregate demand but also upon how changes in
nominal aggregate demand are divided between changes in

---

[1] See Hume, D., 'Of Money', in *Political Discourses*, Edinburgh, 1752, pp. 41–59,
reprinted in Walters, A. A. (ed.), *Money and Banking*, Harmondsworth, 1973.

output and changes in prices. This second relationship itself depends, not upon strictly monetary matters, but rather upon the real factors which determine the elasticity of supply of aggregate production; chiefly the form of the production function, and the institutional conditions in the labour market. Although this is no place to analyse the complexities of these real relationships as opposed to monetary relationships, we must investigate the foundations of certain key ideas—the Phillips curve, the natural rate of unemployment, and the role of inflationary expectations.

Consider a world with a fixed money wage, declining marginal productivity of labour, a fixed and fully employed capital stock, and perfect competition in both product and factor markets. If we begin from a position of unemployment, what effect will increases in aggregate demand have on the price level? Faced with increased demands for goods and services, producers will try to obtain more labour (and other factors). Although more labour is forthcoming at the same money wage, since marginal productivity falls with increasing employment, unit costs of production will rise. Even with fixed money wages, therefore, prices will rise as aggregate demand increases. None the less, if workers are prepared to accept falls in their real wages, then employment will increase. But suppose we hold the level of employment at its new higher level; is there any reason for the rise in prices to continue? On this basis it is clear that there is not. Increases in aggregate demand spend themselves proportionately more in increasing prices rather than output the higher the level of employment, until, at the point where all labour is employed, no increases in output are forthcoming, but the *level* of employment does not imply any rate of change of the price level.

Of course we have to allow for the specialization of factors of production; as aggregate demand increases, excess demands for some types of labour develop even when others are still in excess supply. The wages of the former will rise and if, as is reasonably assumed, the wages of the latter do not fall, then the general level of wages will rise. Moreover, as demand for particular types of labour increases, groups of workers may try to push their wages further up. The stronger these factors are the greater will be the impact of given increases in nominal aggregate demand on prices rather than on output. Nevertheless, *ceteris paribus*, at any given sustained level of real output and employment, the price level will be stable. In short, we have established a relationship between the level of employment and the level of prices but no relationship between the level of employment and the rate of inflation. This is as far as Keynes took the theory of inflation and employment.[2]

In 1958, however, A. W. Phillips published an article in which he claimed to have discovered a stable relationship between the level of unemployment and the rate of change of money wages in the United Kingdom for the period 1861–1957.[3] At least for the succeeding decade this statistical relationship was accepted as revealing a fundamental economic relation of general applicability. Given the apparent ease with which it could be transformed into a relationship between the level of unemployment and the rate of price inflation,[4] it seemed to present the policy-maker with a range of alternative combinations of the levels of unemployment and steady rates of inflation from which he could make his preferred choice. This is shown by the solid curve in Figure VI.1.

In order to understand why this Phillips relationship has broken down, not only in the United Kingdom, but across all of the industrial world, we have to investigate its theoretical rationale.

The classic theoretical explanation of the Phillips curve derives from Lipsey.[5] The level of unemployment can be viewed as a stock, the level of which is determined by two flows—the flow of newly unemployed and (abstracting from growth of the labour force) the flow of previously unemployed workers finding jobs. Now let us suppose that the rate at which the unemployed find jobs depends positively on the excess demand for labour and that the rate at which workers are made

2 See Keynes, J. M., *The General Theory*, ch. 21.

3 Phillips, A. W., 'The Relations between Unemployment and the Rate of Change of Money Wage Rates in the United Kingdom, 1861–1957', *Economica*, November 1958.

4 See Samuelson, P. A., and Solow, R. M., 'Analytical Aspects of Anti-Inflation Policy', *American Economic Review*, May 1960, pp. 177–94.

5 Lipsey, R. G., 'The Relation between Unemployment and the Rate of Change of Money Wage Rates in the United Kingdom 1862–1957: A Further Analysis', *Economica*, February 1960.

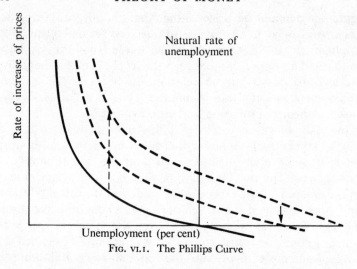

FIG. VI.I. The Phillips Curve

unemployed is unaffected by it. The level of unemployment will then be negatively related to the level of excess demand for labour. Furthermore, since employers and workers will try to eliminate this excess demand by raising money wages and hence prices, the greater the level of excess demand the higher will be the rate of inflation. We now have a link between levels of unemployment and rates of inflation. However, the foregoing argument begs a crucial question. The assumption of declining marginal productivity implies that the real wage falls as employment increases, hence at some point, as we move to higher levels of employment and inflation in line with the Phillips relationship, prices must rise faster than wages. The crucial question' is whether these falls in the real wage are what economic agents want; that is whether they bring the economy closer to equilibrium in the market for labour. If they are, we may expect the relationship between unemployment and inflation to hold good; if not, we should expect agents to try to re-establish equilibrium by increasing the real wage. Now in our earlier Keynesian story we assumed that workers were prepared to accept cuts in real wages brought about by increases in prices rather than by cuts in money wages[6] and there may be

[6] See Leijonhufvud, A., *On Keynesian Economics and the Economics of Keynes*, New York, 1968, pp. 95–102 *et passim*, for a discussion of the possible reasons for such behaviour.

something of an analogue to this in the present context. Suppose that because of continual switches of demand and supply between sectors, in the absence of inflation, some workers are always involuntarily unemployed. Then a continuing constant rate of inflation permits cuts in real wages without money wages having to fall, and the faster the rate of inflation the greater the variability in real wages and hence the higher the levels of employment.

It is doubtful, however, whether this argument can be relied upon, because, in a growing economy, it is possible for relative real wages to change a lot without money wages having to fall. Moreover, the argument assumes that workers as a whole are prepared to accept the changes in relative real wages that the inflation is supposed to facilitate. If they are not, the inflation, rather than moving the labour market closer to equilibrium, moves it further away. If it is the case that workers are not prepared to accept these changes in relative real wage rates (or declines in the absolute real wage rate if we are working with a one-sector, declining marginal productivity model), then we must specify the basis for the increases in employment which, according to the Phillips relationship, are supposed to be bought at the expense of higher, but steady, rates of inflation. This basis can indeed only be money illusion; that is to say, workers are persuaded that the increases in money wages represent greater real wage gains than they actually do. Such gains in employment therefore depend upon workers under-estimating the inflation rate, yet such underestimation cannot continue indefinitely. We must presume that workers are able to learn from experience and thereby adjust their expectations and wage demands accordingly. Once this happens, the only way a given unemployment rate can be maintained below the position of real equilibrium is by the persistence of money illusion through the continued excess of the rate of price infla-tion over the expected rate. Since the expected rate will be continually 'catching up', this effect can only be sustained by continually accelerating inflation where even the rate of acceleration must exceed that which is expected. It will be seen that this acceleration can continue without limit.

Taking the *natural unemployment rate* to mean the point at which the simple Phillips curve (shown in Figure VI.1 as the

solid curve) cuts the horizontal axis, this acceleration of inflation can be represented as a process by which the Phillips curve
shifts up by the change in the expected inflation rate whenever
the unemployment rate is below the so-called natural rate, and
shifts down whenever it is above it. For it is only when unemployment is at the natural rate that economic agents will cease
trying to alter the real wage by securing money wage increases
which differ from the anticipated rate of inflation. As Figure
VI.1 indicates, this analysis can readily explain the coexistence
of accelerating inflation and increasing unemployment.

It is now time to return to our original question of how much
a given increase in the money supply will affect prices and how
much it will affect output and employment. We can now see
that the influence of a given increase in aggregate nominal
demand depends crucially upon the behaviour of inflationary
expectations, which may be uncertain and volatile. Many
models assume a simple error-learning mechanism of expectations formation whereby this period's expected rate differs from
last period's by the difference between last period's expected
rate and last period's actual rate. But, at least in a period of
accelerating inflation, such behaviour appears to be downright
irrational because, since it implies that this period's expected
rate is equal to last period's actual rate, this period's inflation
rate is *always* under-predicted. Moreover, it bases predictions of
the future solely on a mechanistic response to the past, yet it is
surely in the nature of human affairs that the special characteristics of the present influence our view of the future, in a continually developing way. Thus we might reasonably expect the
state of the foreign exchange market, the wage claims of key
unions and even perhaps the current rate of increase of the
money supply to have a bearing on the issue, but not in a way
which can be readily formalized as having general applicability.
As Sir John Hicks has urged, we must beware of thinking of
expectations too arithmetically, for 'if anything happens to
cause the price rise to accelerate (even temporarily) the expectation of inflation lights up, and then becomes an independent
cause of further inflation'.[7]

---

[7] Hicks, Sir John, 'Expected Inflation', *Three Banks Review*, September 1970,
p. 14.

The behaviour of the natural rate of unemployment constitutes another source of uncertainty, for despite its name, it is far
from 'natural', being quite simply that rate of unemployment at
which the labour market is in equilibrium without money
illusion, given all the real and institutional forces which affect
the demand for and supply of labour. Now these 'real and
institutional forces' are clearly subject to change. Let us suppose,
for instance, that in an economy where all of the work-force is
unionized, trade unions as a whole attempt to secure increased
real wages at given levels of employment. Given the usual conditions of profit maximization and unchanged productivity, in
aggregate, they must fail in their objective. But if they persist,
the Phillips relation, which was formerly appropriate, can no
longer be so, for as long as the authorities try to maintain
employment at the old level, the unions will, by assumption, try
to increase real wages by pushing up money wages, thus
increasing inflation.

What effect can money have on this behaviour? If the growth
of the money supply is either fixed at some predetermined rate
or at some rate substantially lower than the rate of inflation,
then increasing demand for money will restrict real aggregate
demand and increase unemployment. If unions reduce their
pushfulness in response to increased unemployment, then there
is an end to this inflationary process. It will come when the
unemployment rate has increased sufficiently to persuade unions
to accept the currently offered real wage which, in a world of
declining marginal productivity of labour and fully employed
capital stock, could rise with increasing unemployment.
Although impact effects and possible repercussions on inflationary expectations render it an incomplete account, under the
conditions set out above we can usefully represent a trade union-
caused cost-push inflation by a rightward shift of the simple
Phillips curve, implying an increase in the natural rate of
unemployment. These results do not require that all of the
work-force be officially unionized. They will follow from only
partial unionization if the power and influence of unions is so
great that non-union wages are effectively tied to union
rates.

Whether unions have such power and influence, and
whether, if they had the power, they would choose to use it, is

the subject of much debate in the literature.[8] Yet, although the empirical relevance of this particular source of disturbance is unsettled, it is but one example of a vast range of chiefly institutional factors which could cause variations in the natural rate. Others include the level of social security payments, the degree of perfection of information in job markets, the degree of mismatching of demands and supplies between sectors of the economy, and the effectiveness of minimum wage legislation. Although Friedman plays down the importance of unions in this context, he urges governments to recognize these factors as causes of unemployment.

There is, however, a further source of variation in the relationship between unemployment and inflation which is exogenous to the labour market, namely changes in import costs. If there is an increase in the price of imported goods this will raise the rate of inflation at existing levels of unemployment, thus displacing the Phillips relationship. If there are no repercussions on wages this displacement will be temporary, but there usually will be repercussions from one or both of two main sources.

The first of these concerns the sensitivity of inflationary expectations. The rise in the rate of inflation, although caused by a once-and-for-all increase in import prices, may lead the public to expect a higher rate of inflation in the future and therefore to press for money wage increases which incorporate an allowance for expected inflation.

The second concerns the inflexibility of real wages. If the rise in import prices is not accompanied by an equal rise in export prices, then the terms of trade deteriorate and real incomes fall. Only if workers accept the full burden of this on their real wages will the rate of inflation remain constant. If, as they usually do, they seek to win back at least part of the decline in real wages by achieving higher money wage increases, then the Phillips relation is more permanently disturbed, for in the aggregate they must fail and hence will need to try again in the next wage round. They thereby present the authorities with an awkward choice between policies which preserve the employment level but validate an increase in inflation, and policies which prevent

8 See, for instance, Friedman, M., *Unemployment versus Inflation*, London, 1975, and Lord Robbins *et al.*, *Inflation: Causes, Consequences, Cures*, London, 1974.

an increase in inflation but reduce employment. Similar consequences may follow even when the rises in import prices are matched by equal rises in export prices (and the terms of trade therefore remain unaltered) if workers are not prepared to accept the changes in the equilibrium structure of relative wages which this implies. Whether or not the terms of trade deteriorate, this more permanent effect of increases in import prices can be likened to the effect of an increase in trade union militancy on the natural rate of unemployment.

In summary then, modern theory has accepted that (over the short run at least) changes in the money supply can affect employment as well as prices, and that together with variations in nominal income velocity, this constitutes an important cause of variation in the relationship between the money supply and the price level. This naturally places the relationship between unemployment and inflation at the forefront of analysis. Our discussion, however, identifies three major factors which may disturb this relationship and thus impart further flexibility to the money–price relation. These are:

(i) changes in expectations of future inflation;
(ii) variations in labour market institutions and other conditions affecting the natural rate of unemployment;
(iii) changes in import prices.

The second and third sources include those generally described as 'cost-push'.

The other task in this chapter is to move to an open economy. Although this is no place to discuss the details of international monetary economics *per se*, we must consider the connections between money and the foreign sector. The effect of opening up our model is to permit trade between nationals and foreigners in both goods and assets. This has two major effects which concern us here; it subjects domestic monetary variables to influence from abroad, and it also moderates the effect of domestic monetary changes on domestic variables. Let us first examine its influence on nominal aggregate demand for domestic goods and services.

The balance of payments can affect the pressure of domestic demand by influencing any or all of three basic variables: (i) the balance of Keynesian injections and withdrawals into the circular flow of income; (ii) the level of private sector net wealth; and (iii) the level of the money supply.

According to the simple Keynesian expenditure/income theory, income is in equilibrium if, and only if, *ex ante* withdrawals equal *ex ante* injections, that is when:

(1) $I + G + X = S + T + M$

Rearranging (1) we get:

(2) $X - M = (S + T) - (I + G)$

According to this condition, therefore, a deficit or surplus on current account can be part of an equilibrium situation, for although an autonomous change in exports or imports sets up forces which tend to counter the original disturbance, the existence of other equilibrating forces prevents the complete elimination of the original change. Suppose exports increase; this raises income which increases imports and may reduce exports. Clearly there is some rise in income which would cause a sufficient rise in imports (and/or fall in exports) to equal the original increase in exports. Indeed, if there were no other leakages in the form of private savings and taxation, this is the rise in income which would inevitably take place. But as income rises, so savings and tax-revenue rise also, thus bringing income into equilibrium before it has risen enough to equilibrate the current account. This implies that deficits and surpluses are not totally self-correcting and therefore that the balance of payments requires deliberate policy action; this will be discussed in Chapter VIII.

It is clear, however, that this model is deficient in at least one major respect—it leaves out the effects of changes in asset positions. *Ceteris paribus*, a current account deficit reduces the money supply and a surplus increases it. These changes in the money supply change interest rates and thus cause changes in aggregate demand which tend to correct the original imbalance. So long as the imbalance persists, moreover, the changes in the money supply will intensify, thus intensifying the changes in aggregate demand and the correction of the imbalance. This can only cease when the imbalance has been eliminated.

None the less, there are two ways in which the adjustment mechanism can be thwarted. The inflow or outflow of money depends not upon the state of the current account but rather upon the over-all foreign balance including the capital account. If a current deficit is financed by an equal capital account surplus, or a surplus by an equal capital account deficit, then the strictly monetary consequences of the imbalance are nullified. The same effect can be achieved, though without the same effect on the gold and foreign currency reserves, if the authorities take the appropriate compensating measures on the domestic money markets. A deficit requires that the central bank purchase government securities for cash, thus expanding domestic credit, and a surplus that it sells securities, thus contracting domestic credit. In some countries there is an automatic mechanism by which such 'sterilization' operations are performed. In the United Kingdom, for instance, the Exchange Equalization Account of the Bank of England acquires and disposes of sterling by the sale and purchase of government securities, thus nullifying the effects of external imbalance on the money supply, but such automatic sterilization can be offset by domestic credit if this is required by the over-all policy.[9]

Let us suppose, then, that such automatic sterilization of monetary outflows and inflows takes place. Does this completely eliminate the effects on aggregate demand? Distribution effects aside, it is clear that, although such action eliminates the variation in money stock, it merely moderates the effect of current account imbalance. A deficit constitutes a withdrawal from the circular income flow and, as it persists, a continuing reduction in private sector net wealth, reflecting increasing external debt; a surplus constitutes an injection into the circular flow, and, as it persists, a continuing addition to private sector net wealth, reflecting decreasing external debt. Sterilization operations merely transfer the changes in asset positions from money to bonds. If expenditure is at all sensitive to wealth level, then deficits will cause an ongoing decline in expenditure, and surpluses an ongoing increase, until the imbalance is corrected.

This seems to return us to the proposition that current account imbalance, at least, will necessarily cause aggregate demand changes sufficient to eliminate themselves, and hence that such imbalances are self-correcting. A glance at equation (2) will,

[9] See Chapter VIII for a discussion of the difficulties of sterilization.

however, cast some doubt even now. Rearranging the right-hand side of equation (2) we get:

(3) $X - M = (S - I) + (T - G)$

This clearly suggests that changes in the government's budget could be used to offset changes in the current account and thus eliminate the effects of current imbalance on aggregate demand.

This discussion indicates the influence which autonomous changes in domestic monetary conditions will have on the balance of payments, and hence the possible role of monetary policy in attaining internal and external objectives. To see the principles more clearly, let us suppose the authorities undertake an open-market operation to increase the money supply.

In the account sketched in the last chapter the rate of interest had to fall until the public was willing to hold the increased volume of money. Now that we have opened the economy, there are foreign assets which can be held as alternatives to domestic assets and any bidding down of rates on the latter will encourage substitution towards the former, hence moderating the fall in domestic rates. The purchase of foreign assets requires the conversion of domestic money into foreign money and, with a fixed exchange rate, an increased demand for foreign exchange necessitates intervention by the authorities to buy domestic currency with foreign. The foreign purchase thus drains the foreign exchange reserves by equal amounts and, unless sterilized, reduces the cash base. The reverse will be true for purchases of domestic assets by foreigners.

The extent of this outflow of funds in response to a fall in domestic interest rates depends upon the substitutability of domestic and foreign assets. In the limit where they are perfectly substitutable their rates cannot diverge from equality, except momentarily. In these circumstances the authorities have lost control of monetary policy, because unless their actions can affect the world interest rate they cannot affect the domestic rate. The only effect of open-market operations is then on the gold and foreign currency reserves, which fall *pari passu* with monetary expansions and rise with contractions.

It is important to see, however, that this limiting case requires more than the mere absence of barriers to capital mobility, for if the nationality of issue of an asset makes any substantive difference to the risks entailed in holding it, then assets of the same general type may carry different rates of interest in different countries. Moreover, there are good reasons for supposing this is so. The first is that, even if there are no controls on capital movements in existence at the time of the contemplated asset purchase, the fear that they may be imposed can still affect capital mobility. The second is that even under a fixed exchange rate system the future exchange rate is to some degree uncertain. Although it is possible to hedge against such risks by taking forward cover, this cover is specific to a certain time period, and if the investor should wish to withdraw his capital before the requisite time he would have to go through the spot market at an uncertain rate. This factor is compounded in the case of marketable securities by the risk that interest rates will change in the future, thus bestowing a capital gain or loss on the holder.

Given that there are such differences in risk between different countries' assets, and given that investors' response to risk is diversification of their portfolios, in a world with a constant stock of wealth we can expect an increase in a particular country's interest rate to induce a once-and-for-all and finite inflow of capital, which will stop short of completely eliminating the increase in the interest rate. Now, granted that it takes time to adjust portfolios, this once-and-for-all stock adjustment will be spread over a discrete period of time, and may appear to be a continuous flow, but must relatively quickly come to an end.

The increase in the rate of interest will give rise, however, to a continuous flow in the opposite direction for two reasons: (i) because, as the amount of borrowed capital increases, so interest payments increase in proportion, and (ii) because, as the rate of interest rises, so the amount of interest payments on a given stock of capital will increase.

When world wealth levels are increasing, an increase in the rate of interest in Country A will increase the proportion of the wealth increments invested in Country A's assets and therefore lead to a continuous inflow of funds so long as the interest differential is maintained. In this case the rate of inflow is likely to be smaller than that during the once-and-for-all stock adjustment in the previous case, but it results in a continuously increasing rate of outflow in respect of interest payments. The long-run effect of a rise in the rate of interest on the balance of payments is therefore negative.

With regard to trade in goods, the direction of monetary effects is relatively certain even in the short run, but the degree of substitutability is relevant to the size of the effects. Ordinarily, an increase in domestic demand increases imports and may reduce exports. An increase in imports unmatched by increased exports raises the demand for foreign exchange, leading to the same sequence as above. In the limit, foreign and domestic goods are so closely substitutable that it is impossible for the domestic price level to diverge from the foreign. If the domestic economy is already at such a level of demand that an increased supply is only forthcoming at increased prices, then all of any increase in domestic demand will fall upon foreign goods and thus drain the reserves. In these circumstances the authorities are unable to raise the domestic employment and price levels.[10]

Substitutability of assets and goods therefore has the same broad effects on the potency of domestic monetary policy. Although the limits mentioned have not yet been reached in practice, growing integration of capital and goods markets increases the relevance of the extreme behaviour which they highlight.

We have seen then that under fixed exchange rates not only is the effect of changes in domestic monetary conditions dissipated abroad, but also these conditions are influenced by conditions abroad. Both of these consequences are avoided by a freely floating rate, and at least mitigated by a more flexible one. Let us suppose that the rate is freely floating and that following upon an increase in the money supply, domestic interest rates fall, causing an increased demand for foreign assets. With a floating exchange rate, the increased demand for foreign exchange must push the rate down until increased supply matches the increased demand, or the increased demand is choked off. Both of these consequences will ensue from both the capital and trade demands for foreign exchange. As the

[10] They may still retain some influence over these levels, however, if, as is usual, wages and prices are sticky over a range of output levels lower than full employment. For then changes in domestic demand will not give rise to price changes and hence not encourage foreign substitution. See Chapter VIII for a discussion of the relevance of this issue to the monetary theory of the balance of payments.

rate falls, investment in domestic assets becomes more attractive, since the comparative returns on holding assets of different countries depends not only upon the relative interest rates but also upon the difference between the exchange rates at the beginning and end of the asset's holding period. For every decrease in the domestic rate of interest relative to the foreign, there is some decrease in the current exchange rate relative to the expected future exchange rate which will compensate. Here the behaviour of the forward foreign exchange market is relevant.

To ensure against the risk of an adverse movement of the exchange rate during the currency of their investments, investors will generally cover their transactions on the forward market; at the same time as they exchange domestic currency for foreign they will contract to exchange foreign currency for domestic (at a specified rate of exchange) when their investment matures. Our increased demand for foreign exchange will force the spot rate down until either the differential between spot and forward rates persuades arbitrageurs, or the differential between current spot and expected future spot rates persuades speculators, to hold domestic assets rather than foreign. Attempted inflows of capital will fail for corresponding reasons; the exchange rate will be forced up until they are discouraged.

In the long run these capital account changes will be reinforced by developments in the current account. As the exchange rate falls, domestic goods become more competitive on world markets, and, given normal elasticity of demand and supply for traded goods, this will increase the demand for domestic currency; *mutatis mutandis* for a rise in the exchange rate.

We have seen, then, that a freely floating rate eliminates the monetary effects of deficits and surpluses and prevents the dissipation of domestic monetary changes abroad. Yet, since a freely floating rate does not necessarily balance the current account, it does not remove the effects of the foreign sector altogether. A current account deficit can still be financed by a capital account surplus, and a surplus by a deficit. Moreover, given that changes in the exchange rate brought about by changes in capital flows affect current account flows, we should note that floating exchange rates enhance the influence of domestic monetary changes and reverse that of international capital flows.

Let us suppose, for instance, that the authorities expand the money supply. Under fixed exchange rates this will undoubtedly be expansionary, but some of the effect will be lost over the exchanges. With a floating exchange rate, however, the attempt to buy foreign assets forces the rate down and thus encourages exports and retards imports.

Contrast this with the effects of an autonomous capital inflow from abroad. Under fixed exchange rates this would, if not sterilized, expand the money supply and have an undoubtedly expansionary effect; under floating rates, it will force up the exchange rate, leaving the money supply unchanged but discouraging exports and encouraging imports.

The insulating effects of floating exchange rates also extend to changes in cost and price levels. A rise in domestic price levels will, under fixed exchange rates, lead to a fall in exports and a rise in imports which will, at least eventually, impose some restraining influence upon the inflation. Under a floating system, by contrast, the rate will simply fall to maintain competitiveness. Similarly, a fixed exchange rate permits the import of inflation from abroad whereas a floating rate prevents it. Both of these statements are, however, subject to the caveat that changes in the capital account may prevent the exchange rate from changing sufficiently to insulate the economy completely.

Although we saw that a floating exchange rate actually reverses the impact of foreign capital flows on aggregate demand, we should note that it also leaves the domestic cost level a prey to the sentiments of the holders of internationally mobile capital. An attempted flight of capital is prevented from lowering the domestic money supply and in the process may even encourage exports, but the fall in the exchange rate which it causes gives an immediate boost to the domestic cost level which may eventually provoke wage claims. Indeed, fear of the consequent inflation may cause such alarm to industry and the public that the net effect on aggregate demand is contractionary.

# VII

## EXTENDED ASSET CHOICE

In Chapter V, we explored a model simplified along Keynesian lines to show the basic principles of how monetary and real forces interact, and Chapter VI dealt with the elaborations necessary to encompass inflation and the foreign sector. The model's chief analytical appeal, the simplicity of its asset structure, is responsible for obscuring many questions of crucial theoretical importance and policy concern. Since the model effectively has only one non-monetary financial asset[1] and no explicit financial sector, there is only one interest rate determined within the system. Questions of changes in the maturity structure of government debt, changes in the portfolio preferences of financial intermediaries, the determination or regulation of this or that interest rate cannot even be asked, let alone answered, within the model's framework. Moreover, although the *IS/LM* approach simplifies and highlights certain basic relationships, yet, without further elaboration, it leads not merely to omission but to downright confusion. It is the purpose of this chapter to elaborate with respect to the extension of asset choice.

Let us consider, for instance, the effect of a once-and-for-all bond-financed increase in government expenditure. According to the model developed so far, there will be a once-and-for-all inflationary effect, due to the once-and-for-all fiscal expansion, but what of the permanent increase in the stock of bonds? Since, *ceteris paribus*, this must raise the rate of interest on bonds, we might be tempted to assume that there is a permanent deflationary effect, yet this only follows once we accept that the rate of interest on bonds can effectively stand for all rates of interest.

---

[1] Although we examined the relative merits of equities as against bonds and money in Chapter III, they effectively dropped out of the analysis because of our assumption (following Keynes) that, in a given state of expectations, the differential between the bond and equity yields was constant.

Let us suppose, contrary to the two-asset assumption, that there is a third asset, equities, whose yield can change independently of the bond yield. If bonds are closer substitutes for money than they are for equities, restoration of portfolio equilibrium then requires an increase in the price of equities which, since it lowers the cost of finance to industry, is undoubtedly inflationary. If, on the other hand, bonds were closer substitutes for equities than for money, then an increase in the stock of bonds would require a fall in equity prices and the effect would be deflationary. The outcome clearly depends upon the substitution relationships between different assets, which is precisely what is lost in our simple IS/LM model by the inclusion of only two assets. Since all models have to simplify to some degree, however, it is worth inquiring as to the appropriate bases for simplification. Following Hicks, we should base our aggregation on the principle that 'if prices of a group of goods change in the same proportion, that group of goods behaves just as if it were a single commodity'.[2] In the case of assets this is achieved by the existence of transactors whose preferences for certain prospective income streams are such that they will be prepared to vary their positions in the assets generating these streams so flexibly that we may legitimately assume that the relative price of the two (or more) assets is constant.[3] We should add that where the substitution links between one class of asset and another are nil then we can safely omit the rates of return on the components of one group from the demand function for any (or all) of the other.

In Keynes's model (and in ours so far) it is implicitly assumed that bonds are perfect substitutes for equities, so that changes in the supply of either equities or bonds must cause changes in the prices of both, and thus that open-market operations would affect bond and equity prices equally. It is similarly implicitly assumed that the sub-categories within this two-asset world (short and long bonds, time and demand deposits, currency, near-monies), are each perfect substitutes for the other components of each general asset category. On the other hand, it is assumed that the substitution links between financial assets

[2] Hicks, J. R., *Value and Capital*, 2nd ed., Oxford, 1946, p. 313.
[3] See Leijonhufvud, op. cit., III.1 and III.2, for a discussion of aggregation procedures and their relevance to Keynes and Keynesian Economics.

(equities, bonds, and money) and real assets held by consumers (houses, land, consumer durables, and human wealth) are virtually nil, so that we can omit the latter when considering the transmission mechanism of monetary changes.

It is worth noting, at this point, that since Keynes, basing his aggregation of assets on differences in maturity, was prepared to aggregate certain near-monies and even short securities with money proper, and long securities with equities, his theory of *the* interest rate becomes virtually inseparable from his theory of the term structure.[4] The reason for this procedure was clearly that, given the problem at hand, his chief concern was the sensitivity of asset prices to changes in interest rates. Since we are investigating the system from a more general perspective we need to disaggregate.

Our task is now to specify the asset structure so as to encompass an analysis of three important issues: (i) the determination of the term structure of interest rates, (ii) the role and influence of financial intermediaries on aggregate demand, and (iii) the disagreement between monetarists and Keynesians over the demand for money, and the transmission mechanism of monetary changes. What we now have to explain and consider is not a single interest rate but rather a whole interest structure 'strung between two poles, anchored at one end by the zero own rate conventionally borne by currency (and the central bank discount rate) and at the other end by the marginal productivity of the capital stock'.[5] We begin by examining the relationship between rates of interest on default-free loans of differing lengths.

Let us first consider in abstract the choice between long- and short-loan contracts from the respective points of view of the borrower and the lender. For the lender, long-term contracts involve the risk of capital loss should it be necessary to liquidate the loan before maturity. On the other hand short-term contracts involve the risk of a fall in income. The latter risk results from the need to renew the loan at the end of each short period during the long period considered, thus exposing the lender to the risk of a fall in income should interest rates fall. Similarly,

---

[4] See Leijonhufvud, op. cit., pp. 150-1, 154-5, *et passim.*

[5] Tobin, J., 'Money, Capital, and other Stores of Value', *American Economic Review, Papers and Proceedings,* 1961, p. 34.

short-term contracts expose the borrower to the risk of a fall in income should the cost of renewing his short-term loan rise. On the other hand, long-term contracts expose the borrower to a capital risk (similar in principle to that borne by the lender) should it be necessary to liquidate the loan before maturity.[6] This risk consists in the capital loss which would be entailed by the borrower buying in his own bonds at inflated prices should the rate of interest fall.

Thus, long contracts involve capital risks for both borrower and lender, and short contracts involve income risks for both borrower and lender. Unless there is some reason for assuming that either income risk or capital risk weigh more or less with borrowers than with lenders we have no basis for a preference by either for short or long contracts as such.

We turn from risk to a consideration of convenience and cost. With regard to both these factors the preference of both lenders and borrowers must be for long contracts rather than short contracts, since both will wish to spread these fixed costs over as long a period as possible. In abstract there is, therefore, no bias in the market as a result of these factors either. We conclude that in principle there is no reason for contending that the risks, costs, or inconvenience of long and short contracts respectively give rise to any preference which is biased as between borrowers and lenders. If a bias is to be explained, in the absence of positive expectations as to future rates, it is necessary to introduce the relationship between the term of the loan on the one hand, and on the other hand the encashment period in respect of lenders and the requirement period in respect of borrowers. This latter we define as the expected period of employment of the funds.

Using these concepts, let us now reconsider the preferences of lenders and borrowers on the assumption that all future requirements are certain. For the borrower, what we have called the capital risk applies only if the term of the loan exceeds the requirement period, and the income risk applies only if the term of the loan falls short of the requirement period. Both risks are therefore eliminated if the term of the loan is equated to the requirement period. Furthermore, cost and inconvenience are

---

[6] This tends to be overlooked, e.g. Kalecki, M., *Theory of Economic Dynamics*, London, 1954, p. 81.

minimized by making the term of the loan as long as possible. It follows from these propositions that, at a uniform rate for all terms of loan, borrowers will prefer to borrow for a term at least equal to their requirement. Except when they are induced by the cost consideration to extend the term beyond their requirement, borrowers will seek to match the term of the loan to the requirement period if the rate is the same for all terms of loan.

For the lender, the capital risk only applies if the term of the loan exceeds the encashment period of the funds and the income risk only applies if the term of the loan falls short of the encashment period of the funds. Both risks are therefore eliminated if the term of the loan is equated to the encashment period. Except where they are induced by the cost consideration to extend the term beyond the availability of the funds, lenders would always seek to equate the term to the availability of the funds at uniform rates.

Now if this matching of the maturity of the loan to both the encashment period and the requirement period could be achieved, then both capital and income risk would be eliminated for both borrower and lender. This clearly requires equality of encashment and requirement periods.

Once we relax the assumption of certainty of requirements and availabilities, however, there will always be some risk carried by borrowers and lenders. None the less, we may still presume that they have expectations about their requirements and availabilities, and therefore borrowing and lending periods over which, in their own view, capital and income risk are minimized. Encashment and requirement periods may then be interpreted in the sense of subjectively estimated minimum risk periods rather than zero risk periods. Risk would thus be minimized for both borrower and lender if encashment and requirement periods were equal.

Following Keynes and Hicks,[7] however, there has been a general presumption that the average length of availabilities is less than the average length of requirements such that on average there is an excess of availabilities in short maturities and an excess of requirements in long maturities—what Hicks

---

[7] See Keynes, J. M., *A Treatise on Money*, Vol. II, London, 1930, ch. 37, and Hicks, J. R., op. cit., ch. 11.

termed, 'a constitutional weakness' at the long end of the market.[8]

This view has not, however, gone unchallenged. Whilst there is clearly no reason to presume that availabilities will be equal to requirements even on average (let alone in each maturity) it is not obvious that requirements will have a longer average duration than availabilities. As Meiselman put it, 'If a constitutional weakness does exist, it is not at all clear which side of the market is, or ought to be, the weak one'.[9] None the less, the rationale behind the presumption of a constitutional weakness at the long end may rest upon the not unreasonable assumption that the maturity of requirements is dominated by the longevity of the capital stock, whereas the maturity of availabilities is dominated by the (shorter) life-cycle patterns of saving and dis-saving.[10] Let us then continue to presume that there is this constitutional weakness. We must now ask how the supply of funds will be equated to the demand for funds in the different maturities.

Suppose that borrowers and lenders were so risk averse that they were not prepared to depart from the exact maturity of their requirements and availabilities on any terms. In those maturities where there was an excess supply of availabilities, rates of interest would then have to fall so as to reduce the supply and encourage the demand. The converse would follow for an excess demand for availabilities. With rates of interest thus adjusting independently in each maturity, the pattern of variation of interest rates across maturities would depend upon the precise maturity distribution of availabilities and requirements. With markets thus effectively segmented, a yield curve relating yields to time to maturity might show humps and troughs, although if the presumption of a constitutional weakness at the long end were justified, it would have a general upward trend as time to maturity increased.

Suppose, on the other hand, that borrowers and lenders were completely risk neutral. Still retaining our assumption of the absence of any positive expectation of a change in interest rates,

8 Hicks, op. cit., pp. 146–7.

9 Meiselman, D., *The Term Structure of Interest Rates*, Englewood Cliffs, N.J., 1962, pp. 14–5.

10 See Leijonhufvud, op. cit., pp. 292–9.

borrowers and lenders would then push interest rates into exact equality, regardless of the maturity distribution of encashment and requirements, for given that the only difference between loans of differing maturities lies in their different capital and income risks, and that by assumption borrowers and lenders are risk neutral, loans of different duration are perfect substitutes.

Now it is obviously highly unreasonable to presume that all or even the bulk of ultimate lenders and borrowers are risk neutral, but this is not necessary to sustain the result. Once we allow for the existence of speculators who both borrow and lend, it is sufficient to assume that a risk-neutral group of these is sufficiently well financed to dominate the market.[11] Under these circumstances, loans of different duration can be aggregated without any loss of information.

It is, however, possible to take an intermediate position in which it is assumed that operators are persuaded to take risks by moving out of their ideal maturities in search of higher expected returns, and thus that the market segmentations are smoothed, whilst still assuming that the system is dominated by operators who remain to some degree risk averse, so that the general slope of the yield curve is influenced by the average relationship between the maturity of encashments and requirements.

If we then continued to presume a constitutional weakness at the long end, the predominant risk to which lenders would be subject would be capital risk. But the same possible range of fluctuation in capital value cannot apply to bonds having different maturity dates because the certain value at maturity places a constraint on the possible fluctuations. This constraint will be the more powerful the nearer the maturity date is to the present. In general the risk premium which a lender will require to compensate him for risk of capital loss must be a function of the range of possible fluctuations. The premium must therefore increase as the length of the loan to maturity increases. We could then conclude that in the absence of any positive expectation of a change in interest rates, the rate of interest would be an increasing function of the length of the loan. But since the longer is the term to maturity the more nearly are two adjacent maturities mathematically equivalent

11 See Meiselman, op. cit., for the strongest defence of this position.

in their price responsiveness to changes in interest rates, the *increase* in risk incurred by a given extension of maturity must diminish as the duration of the loan increases.[12] Under these conditions, the yield curve would be upward-sloping but the slope would diminish as term to maturity is increased. A position of this sort is shown in Figure VII.1.

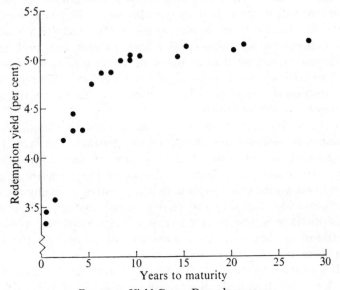

Fig. vii.1. Yield Curve, December 1959

But the possible relationships described above, and the factors contributing to them, are generally obscured and frequently obliterated by the factor from which we have so far abstracted, namely expectations. We must now consider the effect of positive expectations regarding the future level of rates.

Other things being equal, a lender will prefer short lending if he expects rates to rise, since he will thereby have the opportunity of benefiting from the rise in rates, without capital loss, at the end of each short-loan period. Similarly, he will prefer long lending if he expects rates to fall, since he will thereby prevent the fall in rates from affecting his income.

On the other hand, a borrower will prefer long borrowing if

12 See Malkiel, B. G., *The Term Structure of Interest Rates*, Princeton, 1966, p. 59.

he expects rates to rise, since he will thereby prevent the rise in rates from affecting his costs. Similarly, he will prefer short borrowing if he expects rates to fall, since he will have the opportunity of benefiting from the fall in rates at the end of each short borrowing.

Combining these arguments, an expectation of a rise in rates will increase the demand and diminish the supply in the short-loan sector, and will increase the supply and diminish the demand in the long-loan sector. Thus the long-term rate will rise relative to the short-term rate; on the other hand, the expectation of a fall in rates will decrease the demand and increase the supply in the short-loan sector, and will decrease the supply and increase the demand in the long-loan sector. Thus the short-term rate will rise relative to the long-term rate.

The above arguments have to be modified, however, by taking into account the behaviour of the government and financial intermediaries. Whatever the preferences of private borrowers, the government is in a peculiarly advantageous position to permit a divorce between the maturity of its require-ments and its debts, and to do so not necessarily in pursuit of the greatest gain to itself. Especially where the government debt is relatively large, therefore, the balance between the availabili-ties and requirements of private ultimate borrowers and lenders need not determine the total balance in the market.

Moreover, the effects of the availabilities and requirements of ultimate borrowers and lenders can be considerably modified by the behaviour of financial intermediaries. There are many reasons for the existence of financial intermediaries which have little directly to do with the term structure of interest rates. By dealing with large numbers of borrowers and lenders, for instance, they can reduce the average risk of default on loans through being more able to distinguish good risks from bad, and pooling such risks as remain. Furthermore, again by dint of their size, intermediaries are able to reap the gains of specialization in the transformation of typically small ultimate savings into typically large ultimate borrowings. Yet part of the rationale behind the existence of at least some intermediaries consists in their ability to take advantage of differences in ideal maturity. By standing between considerable numbers of ultimate bor-rowers and lenders, and thus pooling withdrawals and deposits, intermediaries can more nearly achieve that matching of the maturity of availabilities and requirements which avoids both income and capital risk, and perhaps through their specialization in financial risk-taking are more prepared to take the risks than are ultimate borrowers and lenders. Intermediaries thus tend to bring rates of interest in different maturities closer together.

None the less, intermediaries are themselves economic institutions and are themselves subject to the same considerations of risk, return, and expectation which we analysed when abstracting from them. In principle, then, their existence does not invalidate the analysis; we simply have to recognize that the hedgers and speculators may be intermediaries, and that the market segmentations may be caused by the maturity preferences of intermediaries, as well as, or rather than, ultimate lenders.

We can, therefore, summarize our discussion by saying that, given the maturity structure of the public debt, the pattern of interest rates prevailing at any time will, in general, depend upon a combination of the expectations factor and the considerations of income and capital risk examined earlier. If there is no 'constitutional weakness' at either end of the market, and if markets are not segmented, or if, even though these conditions do not hold, risk-neutral speculators dominate the market, then the long rate will equal the average of short rates which are expected to prevail during the life of the long bond. If, on the other hand, the system remains predominantly averse to a particular sort of risk, then this relationship will be modified by the presence of a liquidity or 'solidity' premium, and if markets are fairly segmented then it may be appreciably altered by changes in the flow of funds into, and the requirement of funds in, particular maturities. Which of these conditions is, and has been, dominant is an empirical question on which there is a large literature.

As we have just seen, financial intermediaries play a key part in the determination of the term structure; it is now time to give explicit consideration to their role in the determination of aggregate demand. Although great stress is often placed on the differences between banks and other financial intermediaries, since we have already given a general view of their interrelationship in Chapters I and II and since a detailed comparison is beyond our scope, we shall deal with the effects of intermediation in general.

There are two aspects which concern us: (i) changes in the public's lending preferences as between different intermediaries; (ii) changes in intermediaries' preferences as between different sorts of lending. In general, changes in the public's preferences will have effects only in so far as the intermediaries are non-homogeneous. A major type of non-homogeneity, which we examined in Chapter II, is differential reserve requirements; another is differences in lending preferences between intermediaries. This obviously has distributional consequences which may be of interest to the authorities (particularly in the case of mortgage finance) but it may also affect the level of aggregate demand. Since we may treat a change in public preferences in favour of an intermediary which prefers a certain sort of lending as equivalent to a change in the preferences of intermediaries in favour of that sort of lending, we can examine this issue under the same heading as our second aspect.

Let us begin by considering the relevance of an intermediary's choice between holding existing securities and granting new credit, the total of its assets and liabilities being held constant. Suppose, for instance, that a bank switches out of gilt-edged securities and into advances to customers. If the authorities do not buy the gilt-edged (in order to maintain their price) then the sale of gilt-edged by the bank must require an acquisition of finance by their new holders of equal amount. Ultimately this can come from one of two sources: (i) the denial of finance to some private borrowers; (ii) a reduction in desired money holdings. In so far as the funds come from (i) then the increased bank finance of the private sector is exactly counterbalanced by a reduction in other finance, leaving aggregate demand unaffected. Suppose, on the other hand, that the funds come from (ii); provided that the lower rate of interest on loans caused by the new bank loans does not persuade other potential lenders to hold money instead of lending it, aggregate demand will increase. The rise in gilt yields induces the non-bank public to take up gilts which they (ultimately) pay for with bank deposits (probably time deposits). The bank then increases advances, thus transferring the former time deposits into the hands of bank borrowers as demand deposits. Since this increase in advances is not matched by an increase in current saving, it clearly increases aggregate demand. The change in the intermediary's preferences has caused a change in the interest rate *structure* such that wealth-holders are encouraged to substitute other assets for money and deficit units are induced to increase their borrowing. It is thus equivalent to a decrease in the demand for money.

The extent of the increase in advances does not, however, give an accurate representation of the extent of the impact on aggregate demand. If, for instance, some other intermediary regards gilts and advances as perfect substitutes, it will then buy the gilts which the bank sells and cut back on advances to the same extent. The switch in the bank's portfolio is then matched by an equal and opposite switch in the other inter-mediary's portfolio. Alternatively, suppose the new bank advances replace direct finance, so that the reduction in desired money holdings made to finance increased public holding of gilts is exactly counterbalanced by an increase in desired money holding as the banks replace the public as providers of funds to deficit units. The bank action has simply altered the distribution of government and private debt between banks and the public.

A similar analysis applies to the question of changes in the preferred maturity of intermediary investments in securities. Suppose that banks switch out of short government securities into long government securities, and suppose that for the non-bank sector, that is for the public and other intermediaries taken together, longs are close substitutes for loans to the private sector and equities, whereas shorts are close substitutes for money. The rise in short rates will persuade non-banks to switch out of longs and into loans to the private sector and equities. Once again the effect is inflationary; a change in interest rate structure induces a reduction in desired money holdings. Notice, however, that if non-banks viewed longs and shorts as perfect substitutes then the interest effect would be zero. Furthermore, if longs were better than shorts as substitutes for money, and shorts better than longs as substitutes for private loans and equities, then the effect would be reversed.

Clearly the effects of intermediary portfolio switches, and hence of transfers of deposits by ultimate lenders between intermediaries, will depend upon the precise nature of the substitution relationships between the various categories of intermediary assets and money.

Having now relaxed the assumption of constant prices, and extended the range of asset choice, we can return to the specification of the demand for money which we examined under those simplifying assumptions in Chapter III. In that chapter we argued that the demand for money was a function of the opportunity cost of holding it, as represented by the expected return on bonds, and the level of current income. We thus start with $M = f(Y, r)$.

The first elaboration is that, since we now have a whole range of different assets for wealth holders to choose from, we should include rates of interest on all homogeneous sub-sets of the whole range of financial asset which can be identified as being differentiated from one another, as representing the differing opportunity costs of holding money.

None the less, we still face the problems of aggregation to some degree. Whenever it can reasonably be assumed that for several sub-sets of assets, elasticities of substitution are extremely high, then we can combine them into a single asset, with a single rate of interest, without a great loss of information. Besides these various forms of financial assets, wealth also consists of real assets. There are four broad types: houses, consumer durables, durable goods, and human wealth. Although all of these except human wealth are traded on markets, their characteristics differ considerably. Houses and consumer durables yield a service in kind whereas ordinary consumer goods such as food carry no yield. The relevance of a yield which accrues in the form of services instead of money is that unless such services are readily saleable, an economic agent's holdings of an asset with such a yield will be constrained by his desired intake of the particular service which the asset yields. It is worth noting in this context that housing has a well-organized second-hand market as compared to the other assets, and produces services which are more readily marketable, although legal regulation of landlord–tenant relationships may restrict this.

Human wealth consists of the present value of future income from human skills and abilities, accruing in the form of wages and salaries as opposed to profits. In non-slave societies it is impossible to have a market in the capital embodied in human beings, but it is possible for individuals to vary their own human capital by acquiring new skills, or allowing them to atrophy. However, the scope for varying holdings of human capital in the short run is clearly limited compared with other assets.

All of these types of real capital, in common with claims to real capital (equities) which we have already considered, rise in nominal value with the general price level. In contrast to both equities and all financial assets, however, they also carry considerable direct costs of ownership. They all need to be maintained, managed, and protected, and even within each sub-set of real assets are, to some extent, heterogeneous. At least in times of price stability, therefore, there are grounds for presuming that they are not as good stores of general purchasing power as money, bonds, or even equities. In times of inflation, however, for much of the population, they may represent the only safeguard against the depreciating value of money.

Secondly, we must now consider the issue mentioned in Chapter III regarding the relationship between wealth and income in the demand for money. Clearly income and wealth are intimately related. For the community as a whole, wealth is equal to the discounted value of expected future incomes. Income is thus the flow or return on wealth; wealth is the stock which generates the flow. There are, however, two ways in which the ratio of current income to wealth can change: (i) if the relation between current and expected future income changes, as it does, for instance, over the trade cycle; (ii) if the rate of interest, at which expected future incomes are discounted, changes.

It is important to note that if neither of these two alternatives holds, then there is little, if any, difference in positing dependence of the demand for money on wealth rather than current income, for they change in the same proportion. Given that both (i) and (ii) may hold, however, inclusion of both can be justified. This is also consistent with the assertion that money has a special function as the means of payment, and hence that the demand for it responds positively to changes in the value of current transactions. It also reflects the proposition that as total wealth increases, with the value of transactions held constant, wealth holders will demand more money because of its convenience, and money value fixity.

In practice, however, there are problems with the relationship between income and wealth. As yet there are no adequate wealth statistics, so that wealth has to be estimated primarily from current income statistics. Inclusion of both income and wealth may then give rise to econometric problems in estimating the demand function. Furthermore, the income which constitutes the return on wealth broadly defined is not identical with measured income, since many forms of wealth (for example, non-interest-bearing money) yield a return in the form of services consumed by their owners rather than being sold on the market.

Thirdly, we must take account of price behaviour, which we introduced in Chapter VI. Once we allow for changes in prices, we must consider how these might affect the demand for money. It seems reasonable to assume that whatever advances in technology and productivity facilitate an increase in real income will similarly affect the economics of large-scale portfolio management, particularly if the costs of transferring between money and other assets include a large fixed term. On the other hand, the convenience and liquidity provided by money may well be a 'luxury' good with an income elasticity of demand in excess of unity. *A priori*, it is not clear which of these two opposing factors will be the stronger. It is generally taken for granted that changes in the price level, in contrast to changes in real income, raise the nominal demand for money in proportion, thus leaving the real demand unaffected. Indeed it would seem to require some sort of money illusion in order to sustain a rejection of this hypothesis.

The effect of changes in the price level is not to be confused, however, with the effect of the expectation of a continuing rise in the price level. *Ceteris paribus*, the anticipation of inflation lowers the expected return on money relative to those assets whose nominal return is free to rise with the expected inflation (for example, equities). None the less, it should be noted that part of the money supply, like bonds, although fixed in money terms, may carry a rate of interest which adjusts to reflect the rate of inflation. Where this adjustment does take place, at least part of the substitution out of non-interest-bearing money will be into interest-bearing money rather than non-money assets.

Given that the opportunity cost of holding non-interest-bearing money is the *nominal* return on other assets and this rises to take full account of expected inflation (thus leaving the real rate unaltered), we could capture the effect of expected inflation without having to add another variable to the demand function. Since the real return on physical goods is, however, difficult to observe (and in some cases is zero), the rate of inflation is sometimes taken as a proxy for the nominal return on goods. Where nominal interest rates do not fully adjust, moreover, there is a further justification for including the rate of inflation in the demand function.

Despite its obviously Keynesian beginnings in Chapter III, the broad lines of the approach which we have outlined correspond closely to the theory set out by Friedman in 1956.[13] Nor indeed is this surprising, for as we shall try to show, the approach should not be seen as particularly Keynesian or monetarist, but rather as a general formulation within which both positions can be expressed.

Friedman views money as one of five broad ways of holding wealth, the others being bonds, equities, physical goods, and human wealth.[14] The demand for money is then a function of the returns on these different wealth forms, and the total amount of wealth to be disposed of. Given that wealth is not directly observable, however, he suggests permanent income (some weighted average of past incomes) as a proxy, and acknowledging that we cannot easily observe a rate of return on human wealth and that it is difficult for holders to switch between human and non-human wealth, he includes a variable representing the ratio of human to non-human wealth instead of the return on human wealth in the demand function. The only other variable which he considers important in the general analysis is tastes and preferences for different assets.

13 Friedman, M., 'The Quantity Theory—A Restatement', in Friedman, M. (ed.), *Studies in the Quantity Theory of Money*, Chicago, 1956.
14 The following exposition draws on Friedman's 'The Quantity Theory—A Restatement', loc. cit., and his contribution, 'Money, Quantity Theory, in *International Encyclopedia of the Social Sciences*, New York, 1968, reprinted in Walters, A. A. (ed.), op. cit.

It must be remembered that money is demanded by two sorts of holders—ultimate wealth-owners and business enterprises. Ultimate wealth-owners treat money as an asset yielding the equivalent of consumption services, whereas business enterprises treat it as a productive asset yielding services which must be combined with the services of other assets to produce the good or service which the enterprise markets. None the less, for a business enterprise the choice of how much money to hold will depend upon the cost of the funds and the relative returns of other productive services which are both represented by the terms already specified for the demand function. Although for empirical work it proves useful to separate the corporate and personal demands for money by including features of the production function (such as the degree of vertical integration), which affect the relative returns on holding money, in the tastes and preferences term, we can conveniently express the demand for money in an integrated form.

Taking $r_m$ to represent the return on money, $r_b$ the return on bonds, $r_e$ the return on equities, $P$ the price level, $\frac{1}{P} \cdot \frac{dP}{dt}$ (the rate of inflation) as the return on physical goods, $w$ the ratio of human to 'non-human wealth', $Yp$ the level of permanent income, and $u$ tastes and preferences, Friedman then writes the following demand function:

$$M = f\left(P, r_\mathrm{m}, r_b, r_\mathrm{e}, \frac{1}{P} \cdot \frac{dP}{dt}, Yp, w, u\right).$$

On the assumption that a given proportionate change in the price level leads to an equal proportionate change in the nominal demand for money, the price level can be removed from the arguments and the relationship re-expressed as a demand for real balances, as follows:

$$\frac{M}{P} = f\left(r_\mathrm{m}, r_b, r_\mathrm{e}, \frac{1}{P} \cdot \frac{dP}{dt}, \frac{Yp}{P}, w, u\right).$$

Alternatively we can re-express the function in terms of permanent income velocity as follows:

$$\frac{M}{Yp} = f\left(\frac{P}{Yp}, r_m, r_b, r_e, \frac{1}{P}\cdot\frac{\mathrm{d}P}{\mathrm{d}t}, w, u\right).$$

$$= \frac{1}{v\left(r_m, r_b, r_e, \frac{1}{P}\cdot\frac{\mathrm{d}P}{\mathrm{d}t}, \frac{Yp}{P}, w, u\right)}.$$

We can then easily derive an expression in the usual quantity theory form:

$$Yp = v\left(r_m, r_b, r_e, \frac{1}{P}\cdot\frac{\mathrm{d}P}{\mathrm{d}t}, \frac{Yp}{P}, w, u\right)\cdot M$$

There is nothing particularly 'monetarist' in expressing the relationship in this way; we could similarly rewrite the demand function from Chapter III as:

$$Y = v(r)\cdot M$$

There are several factors that we should note about the Friedman expressions. The first is that, although there is an indirect reference to them through the close connection between the concepts of income and wealth, the level of transactions and characteristics of the payments mechanism which play an important part in determining the demand for money in the exposition in Chapter III and in the older quantity theory tradition simply do not appear in the function. The reason for this is clear; Friedman sees the volume of transaction per unit of income and the volume of money required per unit of transactions as themselves a function of the variables included in the expression. It is clearly important, then, that Friedman himself concedes that, 'This does not, of course, exclude the possibility that, for a particular problem it may be useful to regard the transactions variables as given, and not to dig beneath them and so to include the volume of transactions per dollar of final output as an explicit variable in a special variant of the demand function'.[15]

A second notable feature is the aggregation of different assets. The problem of the term structure does not appear and there is no mention of near-monies, nor indeed of intermediary

[15] Friedman, M., 'The Quantity Theory—A Restatement', loc. cit., p. 13.

portfolio behaviour. Moreover, the various sorts of physical goods which we distinguished have been collapsed into a single category, and there is no reference to rates of interest offered on any of these wealth forms held abroad rather than domestically. Once again, however, Friedman acknowledges some (at least) of these difficulties. He writes:

Each of the four rates of return stands, of course, for a set of rates of return, and for some purposes it may be important to classify assets still more finely—for example to distinguish currency from deposits, long-term from short-term fixed value securities, risky from relatively safe equities, and different kinds of physical assets from one another.[16]

Although by no means all monetarists agree with Friedman, his views have been so influential that we shall now use the above discussion as a basis for a comparison of monetarist and Keynesian views on the demand for money. It is more important, however, that this should be a comparison with modern Keynesian views rather than Keynes's own, since it is the current controversy which concerns us, and what Keynes wrote hardly constitutes a hard and fast creed to which Keynesians must adhere for all time. Indeed, in some cases the epithet 'Keynesian' may be quite inappropriate, perhaps 'non-monetarist' would be better. It is particularly important, moreover, not to be misled by the apparently large differences between Keynes's simple demand function based upon motives and Friedman's more general and extended formulation without reference to motives. Indeed, with the reservations we have already made, we can agree with Patinkin's view that, 'What Friedman has actually presented is an elegant exposition of the modern portfolio approach to the demand for money'.[17]

None the less, there clearly are substantive differences between monetarists and Keynesians on the demand for money, but they chiefly consist of differing presumptions about the values and stability of the various substitution relationships in the demand function. In a world where such values could be reliably established by empirical tests such presumptions could

16 Friedman, M., 'Money, Quantity Theory', loc. cit., pp. 440–1.
17 Patinkin, D., 'The Chicago Tradition, the Quantity Theory and Friedman', *Journal of Money, Credit and Banking*, February 1969.

have only transitory significance, for differences of opinion could only exist during the interval between the formulation of an hypothesis and the emergence of the empirical results. It is clear that econometrics does not as yet, and perhaps never will, provide a completely satisfactory method of establishing the truth or falsity of such presumptions. The differences to which we are about to refer can therefore be interpreted either as presumptions held in the absence of definitive evidence, or as theoretical justifications for the differing empirical results mustered on the two sides.

The first substantive difference concerns the qualities of different assets. Keynesians are prone to think that money is simply the most liquid of a wide group of closely substitutable financial assets which are quite strongly differentiated as a group from real assets. They thus believe that the elasticities of substitution between money and other financial assets are much greater than those between money and real assets. Monetarists, by contrast, stress the uniqueness of money and do not single out any particular asset or group of assets as a particularly strong substitute for it. Monetarists thus tend to include a wider range of assets in their demand functions for money, whereas Keynesians tend to exclude some on the basis of a presumed negligible elasticity of substitution. The extreme version of the Keynesian view is of course the 'liquidity trap' in which the elasticity of demand for money becomes infinite. No Keynesian would generalize this as a normal situation and Keynes himself was doubtful whether it had ever occurred, though he then had in mind the 'floor' level of interest rates.[18] The speculative fixation version of the liquidity trap as set out in Chapter V is a plausible special case in the short term, consistent with both Keynesian and monetarist treatment of expectations, but in the general case the issue is the extent to which there is normally some element of the liquidity trap. It is an empirical issue regarding the interest elasticity of the demand for money.

Although Friedman claims that the issue of interest elasticity is not important, he strongly believes that the issue of stability is important. He insists that stability of the demand for money function does not mean strict invariance of income velocity but

[18] See *General Theory*, p. 207.

rather variance according to the values of the variables appearing in its demand function. Now as Friedman notes in his 1956 essay, for the concept of stability of a function to have any meaning the number of variables in the function has to be restricted. If we included all the variables that could possibly affect the demand for money, then of course the demand for money would be a stable function of all these variables, but it would no longer have any useful meaning. Friedman restricts his list of variables to the rates of return on bonds, equities, and physical goods, the level of permanent income, the ratio of human to non-human wealth, the rate of price inflation, and a portmanteau term including tastes and preferences for different assets. But for the assertion of stability of this function to prove contentious, the rates of return on assets and tastes and preferences must be defined more closely; if they are allowed to include rates of return based on expectations of capital gain or loss, as Friedman seems to imply they should, then Keynes himself would presumably have concurred with Friedman's assertion of stability. After all, is there not a sense in which Keynes put forward a theory of a stable demand for money, with bond-holders' expectations of the future course of interest rates as one of the arguments?

Similarly, the portmanteau term, $u$, requires further definition before the assertion of stability acquires any meaning. After all, Friedman acknowledges that $u$ may include feelings of uncertainty about economic stability; whilst the demand for money may well be a stable function of these feelings *inter alia*, the feelings themselves are highly variable.

This is not to suggest that there is no disagreement on the demand for money but rather to emphasize that the disagreement is really an empirical one. Friedman clearly believes that changing expectations about the future course of interest rates do not, as an empirical matter, dominate the demand for money, and also that it is possible to specify and predict the effect of particular disturbances arising at particular times and in particular countries from factors included in $u$.

A further possible source of contention may arise from the non-inclusion of rates of interest on financial assets apparently similar to money, such as building society deposits, and indeed to the total absence of terms relating to interest rate *structure*.

For in contrast to Keynes's own foundation of his view of the variability of velocity on speculative behaviour, Keynesians have tended to stress the continuing process of financial innovation and concomitant development of new money substitutes as being a major destabilizing factor. Although concern about the possibly destabilizing effect of the development of near-monies receded after reaching a peak with the Radcliffe Report, recent experience in the United Kingdom has tended to emphasize the importance of relative interest rates.

Extension of asset choice and reconsideration of the demand for money enables us to consider another issue which the simple *IS/LM* model treats only under very restrictive assumptions, and which is a further source of disagreement between monetarists and Keynesians—the transmission mechanism by which changes in monetary conditions affect aggregate expenditure. In our simple model, changes in the supply of, or demand for, money affect expenditure by changing the cost of borrowing, thus, in a given state of entrepreneurial expectation, encouraging or discouraging industrial investment. We must now draw a fuller and more general picture of the processes at work.

Re-emphasizing the portfolio approach, we must first recognize that wealth-holders will maximize their utility by equating at the margin the rate at which they can exchange assets in the market with the rate at which, given the various merits and defects we have set out, they are just willing to exchange them. Balance sheets are only in equilibrium when wealth-holders have achieved this maximum position, constrained by the total wealth at their disposal.

There are two sorts of disturbance to this equilibrium which must be considered: (i) those which alter the total stock of net wealth, and (ii) those which simply alter its components, leaving the total unchanged. It is not clear, however, which assets should be included as net wealth. We could argue that, since the community as a whole can only hold its wealth in the form of real assets and human capital, the amount of money in the system cannot *of itself* influence this total; money is merely one example of the whole class of financial assets which, since they constitute claims by one sector on another, sum to zero over the community as a whole. The cash component of our

definition of money represents a claim by the private sector on
the government and hence indirectly on itself; bank deposits
are a claim by the non-bank public on the banks.

None the less, changes in the volume of cash would then
affect the volume of the *private sector's* net wealth, and given (i)
that the government responds differently from the private
sector to changes in its wealth position and (ii) that the private
sector does not fully, if at all, take into account the theoretical
implications of government debt being its own liabilities, then a
change in the volume of cash may induce a wealth effect on
expenditure. For this reason, cash has been classified as an
'outside' financial asset.[19]

An increase of government expenditure financed by the issue
of cash (or bonds for that matter), falls into this category, since
no withdrawal of assets from the private sector matches the
addition of new cash. In an open-market operation, by contrast, the authorities withdraw assets equal in value to those
injected.

On the other hand we could argue that cash claims on the
government only constitute net wealth because of the services
which cash provides, and inside money provides virtually
identical services. At the margin the cost of providing these
services incurred by financial intermediaries is equal to the
returns, and for depositors the opportunity cost of deposits must
be equal to the subjective value of the services. But on intra-
marginal units there will be a surplus for both depositor and
intermediary. Since these surpluses constitute flows of income
in money or services, we can argue that increases in the money
supply, whether inside or outside, increase net wealth.

Whether government bonds are to be counted as net wealth
turns on a different argument. When the stock of bonds
increases, the value of claims on the government increases and
this is generally taken to represent an increase in net wealth.
But the present value of a bond represents the discounted value
of future interest payments and repayment of principal by the
government, and these payments, one could argue, must be
financed by taxation. If the public perceives the increased tax
payments implied by the increased stock of bonds, perceived net
wealth will not have increased.

[19] Gurley, J. G., and Shaw, E. S., op. cit.

Despite this argument, the degree of uncertainty involved, the unevenness of implied tax payments across the public, and the possibility that the tax liabilities may not materialize, either because the government deficit finances an investment project, or because the bond issue is subsequently monetized, all suggest that it is highly improbable that an increase in the bond stock would leave net wealth unaffected.

In order to highlight the different effects at work, and to conform to what appears to be the majority view on the subject, let us assume that cash and bonds are to be fully counted as net wealth but inside money is not. Furthermore, bonds comprise the total issued whether held directly by the public or indirectly in the form of claims on financial intermediaries which reflect government debt. Let us suppose that the authorities undertake an open-market operation, buying bonds with cash and thus raising the bond price (lowering the yield). Since, *ceteris paribus*, the increase in the money supply makes other forms of wealth-holding relatively more attractive, the demand for other assets will also rise until higher asset prices persuade wealth-holders to accept the new combination of assets.

These increases in asset prices may induce increases in expenditure via three possible channels. Firstly, despite the wealth neutrality of the actual exchange of assets, the rise in the price of assets left in the system raises private sector net wealth and thus may induce a wealth effect on consumption. Secondly, as the increased demand for alternative assets spreads to real assets, their prices are bid up relative to the cost of new production, thus encouraging an expansion of investment expenditure on capital goods by companies, and houses and consumer durables (the latter being classed as consumption in national income accounting), and, theoretically at least, on ordinary physical goods and the components of human wealth, by households.

Thirdly, the fall in asset yields and corresponding fall in the cost of borrowing may encourage borrowing and dis-saving for pure consumption, although this substitution effect may well be offset, either partially or completely, by an income effect which operates in the opposite direction.

Keynesian analysis of the transmission mechanism has

typically focused on the second channel, and has drawn a distinction within it between purchases of real assets by individuals and companies. The decision to invest by companies, it is argued, needs to be treated differently from portfolio decisions by individuals. There are chiefly two reasons for this. Firstly, ultimate wealth-holders actually buy real assets such as houses, cars, or clothing, but they only buy *claims* to corporate real assets in the form of equities. For expenditure on real assets by individuals to increase it is only necessary that there be some response in price or output by the industries producing those goods; for corporate investment to increase following upon an increased demand for equities it is also necessary that managers of companies take the view that expansion is worthwhile. Under certain highly abstract conditions managers might respond so perfectly to changes in equity prices that their decision-taking role was analytically unimportant. In the real world this is unlikely to be the case.

Secondly, whereas corporate investment goods have to be combined in specialized production processes and the goods produced have to be sold on the open market, consumer investment goods produce services which are more nearly independently consumable, and are consumed directly by the owners. This difference tends to make the profitability of corporate investment more sensitive to uncertainty and changing views about the future. Although all asset purchases are in principle subject to estimation of future returns and thus the concept of the marginal efficiency of capital can be extended to non-corporate investment decisions, Keynesians have emphasized their beliefs about the sharp differences between corporate and individual real asset purchases by reserving the marginal efficiency concept for corporate investment and stressing its high sensitivity to changes in expectations.

Although Keynesians have tended to neglect wealth effects and substitution effects on consumption through time preference, channels (i) and (iii), it is not primarily through an emphasis on these that the monetarist position is distinctive; the main weight of the monetarist case, at least in the dominant school led by Friedman, rests upon the nature and strength of the second channel. By positing money as a generalized substitute for a whole range of assets, real and financial, monetarists are led to suggest that the substitution effect on asset yields significantly affects not only corporate investment but also a wide range of non-corporate expenditure. Because of a presumed high degree of elasticity of expenditures with respect to changed yields, moreover, they believe that these effects are not only general but strong. Furthermore, Friedman and Meiselman suggest that once the price of real assets has increased in response to a monetary expansion, consumers will begin to substitute hiring the services which the assets render for the purchase of the asset themselves (for example, the hiring of cars or use of taxis instead of buying a car).[20] In this way the increased demand spreads to ordinary consumption expenditure. On this basis we can see that according to the Keynesian view monetary policy operates by changing the rates of interest on a few widely traded securities and on flows of credit. Monetarist analysis, on the other hand, includes this as merely a part of a more general rearrangement of portfolios. If we therefore use the terms 'credit' to refer to the Keynesian view, and 'monetary' to the monetarist, we can say that 'the crucial issue that corresponds to the distinction between the "credit" and "monetary" effects of monetary policy is not whether changes in the stock of money operate through interest rates but rather the range of interest rates considered. On the "credit" view, monetary policy impinges on a narrow range of associated expenditures. . . . On the "monetary" view, monetary policy impinges on a much broader range of associated expenditures.'[21]

In the next chapter we will extend this comparison between monetarist and Keynesian views, but first we must examine the theoretical nature of the problems confronting the monetary authorities.

[20] Friedman, M., and Meiselman, D., 'The Relative Stability of Monetary Velocity and the Investment Multiplier in the United States, 1897–1958', Research Study Two in *Stabilisation Policies*, produced for the Commission on Money and Credit, Englewood Cliffs, N.J., 1964, p. 220.

[21] Friedman and Meiselman, loc. cit., p. 217.

# VIII

## THEORY OF MONETARY POLICY

In this chapter we propose to examine the theory of monetary policy in terms of the structure of policy problems, conflicts, and solutions.

Broadly speaking, monetary policy is aimed at the macro-economic goals of full employment, price stability, growth and balance of payments equilibrium, with income distribution as a subsidiary objective. As such, monetary policy is merely one of several weapons which the authorities can deploy to achieve these ends. But, in addition, there are certain goals subsidiary to these in respect of which monetary policy has a special role to play. It is the duty of the monetary authorities to ensure the financing and re-financing of government deficits at minimum possible cost to the Exchequer, because a heavy burden of debt interest payments may have adverse consequences for income distribution, and if financed through taxation could distort the allocation of resources.

It is also incumbent on the authorities to manage the financial system so as to ensure its stability, efficiency, and development in the face of changing needs and opportunities. Furthermore, these ends are to be sought, as far as possible, by means which accord with the importance given to fairness and free enterprise in a democratic, mixed economy.

We should note, moreover, that the goals of macro-economic policy are highly non-homogeneous in their assumed responsiveness to monetary policy. Inflation, employment, and the balance of payments all have clear channels through which they may be influenced by monetary changes, but growth and income distribution are quite different. In general, the tools of monetary policy would appear to be too unspecific to achieve much in terms of income redistribution as compared to fiscal policy, while growth rates of output capacity (as distinct from aggregate demand) remain notoriously difficult to explain (let alone to control) by any method. In so far as growth responds to the pressure of aggregate demand, monetary policy may be able to influence it, but the growth objective would then be virtually inseparable from the employment objective. As such, monetary policy would not have a different role from fiscal policy. However, in so far as low rates of interest affect investment proportionately more than consumption and growth responds to investment, then monetary policy may have a special role to play.

As even a casual inspection of the problem reveals, not all of these goals are mutually compatible, but we should note that such incompatibility as exists is not all of the same kind. The incompatibility which may exist between full employment and price stability will exist no matter what combination of aggregate demand policies is employed, since both employment and the general level of prices respond to a single common demand stimulus—the level of aggregate demand for domestic goods and services. These objectives can only be separated by the use of a policy to influence the prices at which output is forthcoming (such as incomes policy). Other incompatibilities, however, may be resolved by a suitable combination of aggregate demand policies. The examination of how policies may be successfully combined is one of our major tasks.

Another task is to draw attention to the problems arising from the uncertainties of the policy process. Throughout the book we have developed our theory in terms of certain key monetary concepts such as the money supply or the level of interest rates, implying or assuming that these could be controlled by the authorities. Now, although, as we shall see, the authorities can exert considerable influence over most of the key monetary variables to an extent differing according to the circumstances none the less, these variables are not directly under the policy-maker's control. They are intermediate between the variables which he can control, the instruments of policy, such as the level of Bank Rate (or Minimum Lending Rate) or the volume of open-market operations, and the ultimate goals of policy to which we referred earlier. This gives rise to two further problems, (i) which system of monetary control should the authorities employ; (ii) within a given system, which instruments should they use to achieve their ends.

Further questions arise from the diversity of intermediate

variables which the authorities can choose between: various definitions of the money supply, wider categories of liquid assets, domestic credit expansion, on the one hand, or the level of different interest rates and credit conditions on the other. Two related questions need to be asked, namely which of the intermediate variables bears the closest relation to the various goal variables (a problem of indicators), and which of them, if any, can serve as a target of monetary policy.

Before going on to examine each of these questions we must pause to clarify certain points which may confuse the reader. The first is a simple matter of terminology. There is no clear consensus on the terms to use to describe the various elements in the formulation and execution of policy. Some writers use the term objectives, or even targets, for what we have described as goals, and the term indicator is sometimes used synonymously with target (in our sense) and sometimes used to denote the thrust of monetary *policy* as distinct from monetary conditions generally.

The reader should also note the somewhat arbitrary implied definition of what constitutes *monetary* policy as distinct from any other policy. Broadly speaking, we have included under the title monetary policy those policies which are formally under the control of the central bank. But this should not be allowed to obscure either the institutional relationship between monetary and fiscal policy nor indeed the analytical difficulties involved in trying to distinguish between them; for instance we can reasonably ask whether a cash-financed government deficit should be classed as a monetary or fiscal expansion. Whatever it is called, it is in reality a hybrid; it can be regarded as a combination of an orthodox bond-financed deficit (the fiscal element) with an orthodox open-market purchase of the bonds (the monetary element).

Wherever necessary we have avoided the institutional complications arising from the relationship between the central bank and the government by using the term 'the authorities', meaning the central bank and the relevant ministry in concert, yet they need not always be in agreement. As far as the United Kingdom is concerned, there is no scope for an independent policy by the central bank, since formally it is under the Chancellor of the Exchequer's direction, although it doubtless carries great influence in policy-making. In some other countries (the U.S.A. for example) central banks enjoy much greater independence, but ultimately the government is paramount.

Let us turn first to consider the role of intermediate variables in their dual capacity as indicators and targets. The general nature of their role as indicators is obvious enough; throughout this book we have expounded monetary theory in terms of relationships between ultimate goal variables and intermediate variables such as the money supply or the general level of interest rates rather than the central bank discount rate or the volume of open-market operations in government debt. But we must now consider which intermediate monetary variable will serve as the best indicator of the macro behaviour of the economy.

The best single indicator is that variable which is most stably related to one or several ultimate goal variables in accordance with the currently observable values of the variables which enter into the function. It should be noted, however, that the best single indicator is not necessarily the best indication of the future course of the goal variables. It is conceivable that the monetary authorities can obtain more accurate predictions by looking at the course of a number of indicators and weighting them in accordance with their own judgements based upon specific information relating to the current situation. Whether they are able to do this or not is at the heart of the debate about monetary rules which we will discuss later.

If the authorities find a single indicator which is sufficient and over which they can exercise control, they may adopt this variable as a target by setting their instruments so as to achieve that value of the target variable which, according to the functional relationship accepted by the authorities, would lead to the achievement of the chosen value for the goal variable. It is important to understand the rationale for the setting of policy in this way. It must be either that no other information about aggregate demand other than that which is embodied in the target variable can usefully be deployed, or that although such other information could be useful, it is not available in the time period relevant for policy decisions. In this sense then, the best target is not synonymous with the best indicator, but it must be closely related to it. It is the best indicator which is also susceptible to control. It is possible that some variables may be good indicators but not good targets.

The relevance of the target-setting approach to monetary policy can best be seen in the context of a simple $IS/LM$ framework.

Suppose that income is determined in an orthodox $IS/LM$ curve system but that this system is subject to stochastic shocks which the authorities cannot predict. Suppose also that the authorities intend to stabilize income at some predetermined level. In the absence of information about the shocks, there would appear to be no basis for choosing between the alternative strategies of stabilizing either the interest rate or the money supply at the level which, in the absence of the shocks, the authorities believe would achieve the predetermined level of income.

Let us investigate the consequences of these different strategies in the presence of shocks to both the $IS$ and the $LM$ curves.

Referring to Figure VIII.1, let us suppose that beginning from an initial equilibrium at $Y_0$, $r_0$, a leftward shift of the $IS$ curve to $IS_1$ displaces the equilibrium to $Y_1$, $r_1$. If we assume that the authorities act so as to maintain the interest rate during this disturbance, then the interest rate will remain at $r_0$ but

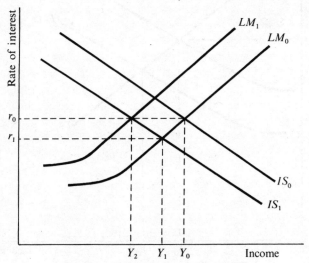

FIG. VIII.1. Target Strategy when $IS$ shifts

income will fall to $Y_2$. It is easy to see that, far from assisting the stability of income, the policy actually hinders it, for in the absence of the reduction in the money supply which is necessary to keep the interest rate at $r_0$, as income fell, the rate of interest would have fallen and thus moderated the decline in income from $Y_0$ to $Y_1$ instead of $Y_2$.

Thus if the authorities had adopted a policy of stabilizing the money supply instead of the interest rate, income would still have fallen but by less than with the interest rate policy. A corresponding argument holds for expansionary shifts of the *IS* curve.

Suppose instead that the system undergoes a shock to the demand for money which in Figure VIII.2 shifts the *LM* curve

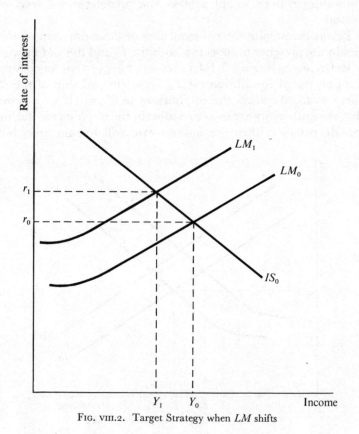

FIG. VIII.2. Target Strategy when *LM* shifts

from $LM_0$ to $LM_1$. If the authorities act so as to keep the money supply constant, then the interest rate will rise from $r_0$ to $r_1$ and income will fall from $Y_0$ to $Y_1$. If the authorities had instead chosen to stabilize the interest rate then income would have remained at $Y_0$. Clearly in this case the policy of stabilizing the interest rate is superior.

In the absence of information enabling the authorities to forecast the impact of shocks, the optimum choice of strategy depends upon the relative size and frequency of the shifts in the IS and LM functions and their relative slopes.[1]

Although it is perfectly conceivable that in particular conditions the interest rate may prove to be the superior target, it is often suggested that in times of inflation this is likely to prove a poor strategy. This is because nominal interest rates, which are readily observable, no longer give a realistic picture of the true cost of borrowing, whilst real interest rates, which supposedly do, are not readily observable, and estimated values require that the authorities be able to estimate the expected rate of inflation. This problem is made even more troublesome if, as has been suggested, the level of desired investment is not insensitive to the rate of inflation even when the real rate of interest is kept constant by changes in nominal rates in pace with changes in expected inflation.[2] In terms of our framework this suggests that in times of inflation the IS curve will be more unstable with respect to the nominal interest than in times of price stability.

By contrast, it can be argued that the money supply strategy is little affected by the advent of inflation because, assuming that the opportunity cost of holding money is represented by the nominal rather than the real interest rate,[3] the money demand function is not destabilized by inflation. Whilst there is some strength in this argument, it can be overstated. Although, under the conditions we have assumed, the money supply strategy would be superior for achieving some specified level of *nominal*

[1] See W. Poole's classic article for the precise specifications: Poole, W., 'Optimal Choice of Monetary Policy Instruments in a Simple Stochastic Macro Model', *Quarterly Journal of Economics*, May 1970.

[2] See 'The Cost of Capital, Finance and Investment', *Bank of England Quarterly Bulletin*, June 1976.

[3] Bailey, J., 'Welfare Costs of Inflationary Finance', *Journal of Political Economy*, April 1956.

aggregate demand, nominal aggregate demand is only of ultimate significance to policy-makers when the price level is stable, which of course, by assumption, it is not. If the authorities are indeed to aim at a specified level of *real* aggregate demand, then again they will have to estimate the expected rate of inflation, for this is a crucial determinant of future inflation and hence of the effect of a given rate of increase of nominal demand on real output and employment.

It is not profitable, however, to pursue these issues further, since they all stem from the assumption that the flow of information available to the authorities is restricted to that contained in the quantity of money and the level of the nominal interest rate. In practice there is likely to be a wealth of other information available. On the monetary side there will be information on the composition of bank assets and the relationship between a whole set of interest rates and asset prices to which the concept of 'the' rate of interest is, as we saw in Chapter VII, a very imperfect approximation. On the real side, moreover, although there will not be information on the current (still less future) level of G.N.P., there will be information on important components and indicators of it, such as car sales, new housing starts, investment intentions, and inventory levels. It is not unreasonable to assume that the authorities may be able to make some use of this information to determine the nature of the disturbances to the system.

In opposition to this eclectic approach, Friedman has declared his support for the view that our knowledge of the magnitudes involved in key economic relationships and of their lag structures is so weak that any attempt to fine tune the economy is likely to lead to destabilization. In its most rigid form, this is a much stronger proposition than that the authorities should not make use of other information when setting their monetary target; it implies that the appropriate monetary target should be maintained regardless of any observed variations in other indicators. For Friedman the optimum target would be a specific rate of growth of the money supply and the only role for new information would be to influence the way in which the instruments were set to achieve this.

The merits of this approach can only be decided by detailed empirical analysis, not only of the stability of the demand for money and desired expenditures, but also of the use made of information by the authorities in trying to correct for instability. However, a casual inspection of the evidence on the demand for money in the United Kingdom suggests that it would require a truly unbelievable amount of destabilization from other sources of information to make the fixed-rule approach desirable. At a more general level, moreover, such a rule must be questioned because it assumes a degree of fixity about monetary relationships which is out of keeping with the observation of monetary behaviour.

At the other extreme the authorities could consider re-setting the target whenever new information came in. Under such a system, however, the authorities would not be operating a monetary target in any acceptable sense of the word.

A further issue, related but conceptually distinct, is whether, having decided on their attitude to new information, the authorities should announce their objectives for the intermediate variable or variables to the public. The advantage of announcement is that it may reduce uncertainty in the financial markets by making clear at least the intended course of the intermediate variable though not necessarily the course of the instrumental variables. The disadvantage is that the announced target must be adhered to if it is to have the effect of avoiding uncertainty, and will thus restrict the authorities' ability to change course on the receipt of new information. This disadvantage clearly does not apply to the Friedman fixed rule or to any other target which is to be firmly adhered to, and in this case the authorities may as well announce their objective.

In the more general case, the length of the period for which the target is intended is crucial; if it is so short that no new information can become available, then the restrictive effect is zero, but so is the gain in stability from announcement. The more the length of the period is extended the greater are both the restriction and the stability.

A further possible gain from announced targets in terms of money growth, which is probably the most relevant one in times of inflation, is that by announcing a target for the rate of growth of the money supply, the authorities give notice that, if inflation rates higher than those expected increase the nominal demand for money, then the consequent decrease in real

demand and pressure on employers to reduce their labour force
will be allowed to take its course. To the extent that wage-push
is an active cause of inflation, such announcements might
perhaps do something to dampen trade union 'militancy' and
hence temper inflation without causing unemployment.

Whether union militancy is an active cause of inflation or
not, announced targets may moderate inflationary expectations
if the public have accepted the diagnosis that there is a strong
link between the current rate of increase in the money supply
and future rates of inflation.

Despite the complications of targets and indicators just discussed, in the highly abstract world we have been considering,
the domestic policy problem is relatively simple; it is merely to
manage aggregate demand so as to achieve the desired balance
between the level of employment and the current rate of
inflation. Moreover, in addition to monetary policy, the
authorities have fiscal weapons at their disposal to tackle this
single goal. Before going on to consider the complications of
additional goals we should pause to compare the relative
efficacy of monetary and fiscal policy for controlling aggregate
demand.

A simple *IS/LM* approach teaches us that for any given
change in aggregate demand resulting from a monetary change,
there is some fiscal change which would achieve the same result.
Why, then, should the authorities prefer one to the other?

In general there are three dimensions to the choice: (i) the
relative size of the multipliers attaching to each policy (the
expenditure multiplier and the money multiplier); (ii) the
characteristics of the time-lag between the implementation of
the policy and its effect on aggregate demand (timing); (iii)
the stability of both the size and timing of the multipliers.

The size of the multiplier is only of relevance if there are constraints on the size of the dose, and timing is probably a good
deal more important. There are two characteristics of the time-
lag: the total length of the period it takes for a policy to have
full effect, and the distribution of the effect over that period.
It would be wrong to conclude that the better policy is necessarily the one which has the largest effect in the shortest time;
the problem is one of getting a policy to operate as nearly as
possible with the optimum phasing for the particular situation.

The third dimension of relative policy effectiveness, stability, is closely connected with this. Whatever the advantages of one policy over another in terms of size and timing *on average*, it could still be reasonably judged inferior if its performance in either or both of these dimensions varied relatively more than the other's.

Once we open up our economy, however, we have to allow for the different effects of the two policies on trade and capital flows, for the policy-maker's task is now to combine his policies so as to achieve simultaneously a domestic demand goal and a balance of payments goal. As Tinbergen pointed out,[4] the simultaneous achievement of different goals requires that the policy-maker has at least as many independent policies as goals, so let us consider the simple case where he can use both monetary and fiscal policy to achieve so-called internal and external balance under a fixed exchange rate.

This is the case examined by Mundell in a classic article published in 1962.[5] Mundell argued that, although both policies affected both goals, such that a monetary contraction operated to counter a balance of payments deficit would vitiate a fiscal expansion aimed to counter a depression, as long as the two policies have different relative effects on the two goals, they can be combined so as to achieve both objectives simultaneously.

Consider an expansion of the budget surplus and an increase in the interest rate, which have the same effect on aggregate demand. Although the two policies would lead to the same reduction in imports of goods and services, the higher interest rate would cause an inflow of capital whereas the increased budget surplus would leave the capital account unaffected. Thus, Mundell argues, monetary policy has a greater effect on the balance of payments.

This is represented graphically in Figure VIII.3, where FF represents the schedule of external balance and XX internal balance (the preferred level of aggregate demand for domestic goods and services). The greater relative effect of monetary policy on the external account is shown by the steeper slope of the FF schedule.

[4] See Tinbergen, J., *On the Theory of Economic Policy*, Amsterdam, 1952.
[5] See Mundell, R. A., 'The Appropriate Use of Monetary and Fiscal Policy for Internal and External Stability', *I.M.F. Staff Papers*, March 1962.

The diagram clearly shows that if the authorities can achieve the unique combination of values for the budget surplus and the interest rate given by the intersection of the two schedules, they can achieve both internal and external balance. If policy

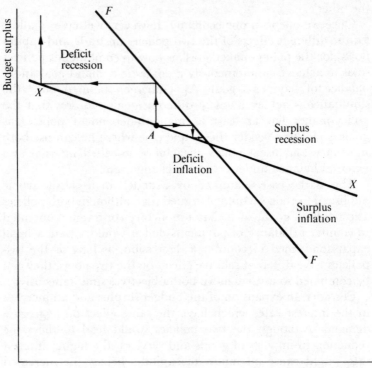

FIG. VIII.3.  Internal and External Balance (Fixed Exchange Rate)

makers were sure of what these values were, the issue would then be quite straightforward, but we have already seen that they cannot reasonably be expected to be sure. The question then again arises of what strategy they should adopt to make the most use of information and minimize the possibly destabilizing effects of their ignorance.

Mundell argues that they should assign each policy to the goal on which it has the greatest *relative* effect, which he terms the Principle of Effective Market Classification. In this case then, monetary policy should be assigned to the achievement of external balance and fiscal policy to internal balance.

Consider Figure VIII.3. Let us suppose that we begin a policy round with the economy at point A. If the authorities set monetary policy in accordance with the internal objective and fiscal policy with their external objective, the economy would take the north-westerly path marked on the diagram. This clearly leads the economy progressively further and further away from the point of internal and external balance.

Now suppose that we reverse the pairing. The economy will then be brought closer and closer to the point of internal and external balance along the south-easterly path marked in the diagram. The moral is thus a simple one: the pairing of monetary policy with external balance and fiscal policy with internal balance is a stable assignment whereas the reverse is not.

Whilst this model of Mundell's has proved illuminating, it is subject to several criticisms. Firstly, the external balance which the analysis makes compatible with internal balance is not balance of the current account. Although this need not be important in the short run, in the long run, borrowing from abroad is unsustainable at constant interest rates, and from a welfare point of view is undesirable.

Secondly, the stability of Mundell's assignment of policies to goals depends upon the FF schedule being steeper than the XX schedule. If increased interest payments outweighed the capital inflow, or if fiscal changes had a strong impact on the interest rate, then the XX schedule might be steeper. 'Because of this possibility, the appropriate assignment cannot be specified according to the relative policy effect criterion without full knowledge of the structure of the economy. If the authorities possessed such knowledge, of course, there would be no reason to assign instruments to targets.'[6]

Thirdly, Mundell investigates stability under highly restrictive assumptions; policies are varied one at a time, one of the two goals is achieved (but not overshot), before the other is pursued, and the position of the schedules remains fixed. In the real world, the schedules are changing markedly, policy changes

[6] Levin, J. H., 'International Capital Mobility and the Assignment Problem', *Oxford Economic Papers*, March 1972, p. 59.

under- or overshoot their objectives, and particular policy problems are so pressing that the knowledge that a certain assignment of policies to goals would eventually lead to a convergence on equilibrium if the schedules were fixed is unlikely to be of much comfort to governments.

We have so far assumed that the exchange rate is fixed. Once we allow it to vary, the authorities have an additional policy weapon, which, if they are free to vary fiscal and monetary policy independently, enables them to achieve a third objective, such as the division of national output between consumption and investment. Since the usefulness of this extra policy weapon is, however, open to question, let us analyse the position assuming that monetary and fiscal policy constitute a single weapon and that the authorities' objectives are again restricted to internal and external balance.

The resolution of this problem is most conveniently demonstrated by the Swan diagram[7] (represented in Figure VIII.4). The diagram depicts combinations of the ratio of foreign to domestic costs and the level of real domestic expenditure which form the loci of the internal and external balance schedules. The diagram assumes a given level of capital flows; monetary and fiscal policy operate by affecting the level of real domestic expenditure and exchange rate changes by altering the cost ratio (a devaluation raising the rate, an up-valuation lowering it). Just as in the earlier cases, the two schedules define four zones of 'economic unhappiness'.

It is clear from the diagram that, except where the economy happens to be located on either the horizontal or vertical line, it requires changes in both the exchange rate and domestic real expenditure to achieve internal and external balance, or, in more general terms, both 'expenditure switching' and 'expenditure reducing' (or increasing) policies. The details of this approach need not concern us here, it is sufficient to notice that this generally accepted approach to the problems of internal and external balance gives the exchange rate a vital role to play and does not support the view that monetary policy

[7] See Swan, T. W., 'Longer Run Problems of the Balance of Payment', in Arndt, H. W., and Corden, W. M. (eds.), *The Australian Economy*, Melbourne, 1963.

is solely responsible for problems of imbalance and solely able to cure them.

This is, however, precisely what the currently popular monetary approach to the balance of payments suggests. The monetarist approach sees the balance of payments as a purely monetary phenomenon; in the extreme, deficits and surpluses are caused by too much or too little monetary expansion and can only be corrected by a reversal of monetary policy. More importantly, the approach claims that devaluation works solely through deflating the real value of the domestic money supply and is thus equivalent to a policy of monetary contraction. If this view is accepted then alterations of the exchange rate no longer provide the authorities with an extra weapon; they become merely a substitute for monetary policy. Let us investigate the basis for such an argument.

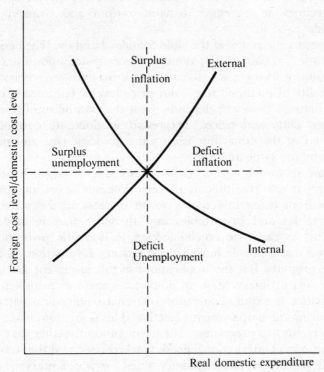

FIG. VIII.4. Internal and External Balance (Flexible Exchange Rate)

Following Hume, the accepted explanation of deficits on the
balance of payments has been that an expansion of domestic
demand causes domestic prices to rise and thus encourages
substitution of cheaper foreign goods. Deficits therefore went
hand in hand with decreases in the foreign to domestic cost ratio,
and surpluses with increases. Under the gold standard mechanism of adjustment, moreover, the imbalance would reduce the
money supply in the deficit country and expand it in the surplus
country. These changes in the money supply would then reduce
the deficit country's price level and raise that of the surplus
country, thus eventually restoring the original cost ratio and
bringing the balance of payments back into equilibrium. It was
the assumption of downward price and wage rigidity, or at least
imperfect downward wage and price flexibility which rendered
this explanation unacceptable. The theory was then modified
by recognizing that if prices and wages did not fall in response
to declines in aggregate demand, output and employment
would.

The abandonment of the Gold Standard and the 'Keynesian'
revolution in balance of payments theory rested upon the substitution of changes in exchange rates between currencies for
flexibility of domestic wage and price levels. The success of a
devaluation, however, depends upon the possibility of raising
foreign costs and prices, (expressed in domestic currency),
without at the same time raising the domestic cost and price
level by the same amount.

Now it would appear to be reasonable to argue that in
general it may be difficult to keep domestic wage and price
levels from rising in response to an increase in the prices of
exportables and importables and therefore that it may be
difficult to raise the crucial foreign to domestic price ratio.
Indeed many people have argued against devaluation on just
these grounds. But the implications of this argument are that
some sort of intervention in domestic wage and price setting
behaviour is required to restore external equilibrium without
impairing the employment objective. This is far from what the
monetarists are suggesting. Their contention is rather that the
integration of international goods markets is so great that traded
goods prices are virtually determined on world markets. An
expansion of domestic demand thereby spills over into increased

imports without first causing any increase in the price of domestically produced traded goods. Thus far, the argument is relatively unexceptional but for completeness it requires that non-traded goods prices be similarly unaffected.

This would follow if the degree of substitution of traded for non-traded goods and the mobility of factors of production between the two sectors were so great that the price ratio of traded to non-traded goods could effectively be taken as fixed. The effect of this argument is that the economy would always lie on the horizontal line in Figure VIII.4, and therefore the authorities would require only policies which affected the level of domestic expenditure (as distinct from expenditure switching policies) to achieve both internal and external balance.

The monetarist position would also be sustained, even though substitution processes worked imperfectly and the ratio of non-traded to traded goods prices therefore rose with an expansion of aggregate demand, if non-traded goods prices were equally flexible downwards. In this case an expansion of domestic demand would push the economy off the horizontal line in Figure VIII.4, but an equal contraction of demand would exactly restore the original position, thus once again rendering an expenditure reducing policy sufficient for the attainment of both goals.

Neither of these arguments seems very reasonable. Whatever its possible relevance for the long run, the first requires a truly remarkable degree of substitution for the assertion to hold good for the sort of short run which is relevant for policy decisions, whilst the second relies on just that downward flexibility of wages and prices which we have come to regard as empirically non-existent.

Given their denial of the usefulness of exchange rate adjustments for reconciling internal and external balance, it may seem paradoxical that monetarists typically advocate floating exchange rates. None the less, there is a clear justification, in that although exchange rate changes are taken to be the equivalent of adjustments in the money supply, yet it may be difficult to pursue an independent monetary policy under a fixed exchange rate, and hence to control the level of unemployment and the rate of inflation.

To understand the basis of this argument, consider a country with an over-all surplus on the balance of payments. As we have seen, this will, in the absence of countervailing measures, inflate the domestic money supply and promote domestic inflation. If the authorities wish to restrain domestic inflation by monetary means they must use the various monetary instruments at their disposal to 'neutralize' or 'sterilize' the monetary inflow. In a world of capital immobility this is relatively easy, but when capital is highly mobile it becomes a good deal more difficult. The problem is that an inflow of capital which is allowed to have full effect will set up forces which will eventually stem the inflow (falling interest rates, rising prices, and poorer prospects of currency revaluation), but that prevention of this equilibrating mechanism will leave the incentive to move in funds relatively unimpaired. In the limiting case of perfectly elastic supply of funds at a given world interest rate, the authorities face an infinite influx of funds if they attempt to hold the domestic interest rate above the world level.

But, even when capital is perfectly mobile, there will not be an infinitely elastic supply of capital to a given country. Indeed, this follows directly from the portfolio considerations explored in Chapter VI. It is true that if the authorities undertake the appropriate sterilization measures successfully the domestic rate of interest will remain above the world level and thus maintain the incentive for capital inflow, but, as the funds accumulate, the proportion of portfolios devoted to investment in this one country will rise. Consequently, continually increasing interest rates will be required to maintain the inflow. The domestic authorities would thus have some independence in domestic monetary policy.

The above argument has prompted some writers to suggest that a high degree of capital mobility does not present any real problems for the monetary authorities so long as the appropriate sterilization measures are taken.[8] Although it has some force, this never the less neglects the complexity of asset structures which we outlined in Chapter VI. Suppose all of the inflow of funds sought employment in government securities. The limit on the extent to which the capital inflow can be absorbed is set

[8] See, for instance, Scott, I. O., and Schmidt, W. S., 'Imported Inflation and Monetary Policy', *Quarterly Review of the Banca Nazionale del Lavoro*, December 1964.

by the sum of the stock of government securities held by the central bank plus the issue of new government securities to the private sector to finance the whole borrowing requirement. However, only if the additional demand were confined to government securities and exactly matched the maturities available would the existing rate and interest structure remain unchanged. But if (as is likely) different maturities of government debt or certificates of deposit, private securities, loans to companies, or equities are demanded, then the inflows of funds can only be sterilized at the expense of a drop in the price of government stock and a change in the rate structure. Although it is difficult to tell how important this factor might be *ceteris paribus*, it will not be welcomed by the authorities.

An alternative strategy is clearly to impose controls on the banks by, for instance, raising reserve ratios either on all deposits or on deposits owned by foreigners. If need be, incremental reserve ratios could be imposed at 100 per cent, so that all of the increase in the banks' cash would be sterilized. None the less, there are still difficulties. Although such a policy would prevent a multiple expansion of bank lending, it would not remove the one-for-one increase in the money supply, reflecting the inflow, unless the authorities were in a position to offset this also. Failing this there would be some bidding up of the prices of domestic assets.

This last problem proved particularly troublesome in the Federal Republic of Germany, where, despite stringent measures on banks to discourage them from attracting foreign deposits, the balance of payments periodically showed a massive surplus mainly in unrecorded items. The explanation appears to have been that German companies were borrowing directly from abroad and thus bypassing the controls on banks. Although the Government's measures had prevented an expansion of bank credit, they left a fringe of unsatisfied borrowers who, at going rates of interest, were able to find finance from abroad.

When faced with a situation of this sort there are two further policies which the authorities may seek to deploy—forward exchange intervention, and direct controls on capital movements. We saw in Chapter VI that the incentive to move funds across the exchanges depended not only upon relative interest rates, but also upon the relation between spot and forward rates. Now although under a fixed exchange rate system the authorities are not free to vary the spot rate (except within the comparatively small permitted fluctuation bands), they are free to influence the forward rate. In order to deter an inflow of funds they must sell domestic currency forward in an attempt to create or enlarge a forward discount or reduce a forward premium; in order to encourage an inflow they must buy domestic currency forward in order to create or increase a forward premium or reduce a forward discount. The difficulty with such a policy is that under a fixed exchange rate system it is usually very obvious which way the exchange rate will move if it is to move at all. It may then prove very difficult to persuade the market to change its views.

Under these circumstances, the only option left to the authorities if they are to maintain a fixed rate whilst being unable or unwilling to sterilize through open-market operations or bank controls is the direct regulation of capital movements.

We shall now consider methods of monetary control. The number of systems of monetary control is potentially infinite, and the most appropriate for any country at any given time will embody those particular institutional characteristics which suit the conditions of the time. In a sense, then, the question as to which system of monetary control is optimal can only be answered in a particular historical and institutional context. None the less, although we shall look at the various systems adopted by the Bank of England in Chapter IX, something can be said about the problems in general terms.

At the most basic level the first choice facing the authorities is whether to operate via market mechanisms or to operate via direction, but the alternatives are not clearly separated, and any practical system is likely to embody elements of both. At one extreme, for instance, the authorities may choose to operate simply by altering their purchases and sales of various types of securities and by varying the terms on which central bank lending is available to the banking system, on the assumption that there is some relationship between these instruments and the monetary variables the authorities are trying to affect, such as the money supply or credit conditions. There is indeed *some* sort of relationship via banks' prudential cash and liquidity ratios and interest rate setting behaviour, but in practice the authorities feel that they can gain greater predictability in these relationships by constraining the banks to hold some fixed minimum ratio of specified assets to deposits or by subjecting certain of their interest rates to official control. At the other extreme, the authorities could conceivably undertake the complete direction of either the borrowing or the lending sides of bank business, or indeed of both, but this could not persist for long unless the banks came into public ownership. Nationalization has occurred in some 'mixed economies' and in most countries (including the United Kingdom) the central banks have, from time to time, given directions involving differing degrees of constraint but left the banks with some considerable leeway to operate on market principles.

Despite the practical overlapping of the two approaches, they do have distinct advantages and disadvantages.

In a completely market-dominated system of control the central bank must accept the allocation of credit which the market determines. If it wishes to alter market conditions generally, it must effect (and be prepared to accept) changes in rates of interest, in particular changes in the rates of interest on the securities in which it trades. But this will not necessarily alter allocation, and if it does the change may not be in the desired direction. The instruments of policy are essentially pervasive and cannot be expected to get at particular sorts of credit which the central bank wishes to influence (for example, credit to exporters or mortgage finance). For these reasons, then, some sort of direct intervention would appear to be desirable.

Direction of financial institutions carries dangers, however, which are both economic and political. If the authorities choose to give directions they must choose which institutions to give directions to, and in precisely which form to give them. As we stressed in Chapter VI, intermediation is an activity which provides benefits to the community. Like the rest of industry, under certain general conditions its resources will be best allocated, and its progress best encouraged, by competition. It is not clear that the authorities can operate a system of monetary control based on direction and simultaneously ensure these objectives.

On the political side, the danger is that a centrally directed financial system may be constrained to lend to the government on terms and in amounts of the government's own choosing, thus disguising the effects of what might be a wasteful redirection of funds from private to public uses. It should be noted that, although this is clearly related to the issue of bank nationalization, it is not identical. The issues which we have discussed concern the degree of competition and independence from central control rather than that of *ownership*. Theoretically at least, a publicly owned banking system could be competitively organized and free from central direction.

Although it is possible to have discriminatory directives with regard to bank liabilities, directives are most commonly issued with regard to bank assets. The justification for such directives may rest on considerations of either distribution of funds or aggregate demand management. The allocation objective can be achieved either by the obvious encouragement of finance for particular sorts of private borrowers (for example, exporters) or by restricting lending to the less preferred borrowers. Furthermore, the authorities may direct the banks to restrict their lending to private customers in general within specified limits, the result being (*ceteris paribus*) that more will be lent to the government. This will not only improve the price of gilt-edged, which, from the authorities' point of view is desirable in itself, but will also constrain aggregate demand.

This constraint of aggregate demand operates through two quite different channels. Firstly, in so far as the authorities are loath to restrict the supply of money for fear of the consequences for gilt-edged prices, the ability effectively to enforce purchases of gilt-edged by the banks may enable them to pursue a more contractionary policy.

Secondly, it is possible to make out an argument connecting the volume of bank advances with aggregate demand. The foundation for this argument was laid in Chapter VI. When banks switch from holding advances to government securities, with the volume of government securities held constant, one section of the non-bank public is denied finance but another acquires surplus funds to the same degree. If the second section could advantageously lend to the first at the same rate of interest which the banks charged, then the effect of the bank switch would be nil. Yet it is reasonable to assume that financial intermediaries have an advantage in borrowing and lending such that a higher rate of interest would be required by an outside private lender. If some other (uncontrolled) inter-mediary cannot be found to fill the need, then some of the original borrowing will be discouraged and the surplus funds held as money balances. This is definitely deflationary, even though the supply of money is held constant. In this way then, the control of the volume of advances may be a method of influencing the demand for money, as distinct from its supply.

If the authorities choose to operate a basically market-oriented policy of influencing the level of deposits, then they have to choose which class of bank asset should act as the fulcrum of control and which instruments they should use to operate on it. In general, any class of assets will do provided that:

(i) the authorities control the total supply of it;
(ii) there is a stable relationship between the total supply and the amount in the hands of the banks;
(iii) there is a stable relationship between the amount in the hands of the banks and the volume of their deposits.

As we showed in Chapter II, cash can be made to fulfil all three conditions. Since the many possible alternatives are heavily dependent upon institutional context, however, it is not worthwhile to discuss their efficiency in general terms. Instead we shall discuss the various alternatives adopted by the Bank of England, in the next chapter.

It is now convenient to extend Chapter VII's comparison between monetarism and Keynesianism in terms of the demand for money and the transmission mechanism to a comparison of views on monetary policy. It should be made clear at the outset that, as in our comparison on the demand for money, there is something artificial about a comparison between monetarist and Keynesian views on monetary policy, since neither is a set of very well-defined propositions which individual theorists either support or oppose *in toto*, but rather a group of rather vague theoretical presumptions which can easily be accepted or rejected in part. Some Keynesians may thus agree whole-heartedly with some monetarists on particular issues whilst being at loggerheads on others. Nor is it the case that the positions of the two schools have remained static over time. It is particularly important, for instance, to distinguish between Keynes's own views and those of later Keynesians, as Leijonhufvud has demonstrated.[9] Moreover, the focus of dispute changes over time; in the forties and fifties, with memories of the Great Depression still fresh, questions of under-employment equilibrium and the role of wage and price flexibility were of great importance, but in the succeeding years these issues faded from the forefront to be replaced by questions concerning the policy problems of managing the trade cycle, and dealing with inflation and balance of payments problems.

Despite the difficulties involved in such a general discussion, the battle-lines are sufficiently well-drawn between the schools, and the issues important enough, to provide a justification.[10] Let us then compare the two schools with a view to discovering the source and nature of the chief areas of dispute.

The difference in beliefs about the size of the general interest elasticity of the demand for money, combined with a difference over the presumed degree of sensitivity of expenditures to changes in interest rates (Keynesians believing in low, monetarists in high sensitivity), establishes different views about the relative size of the money and autonomous expenditure (Keynesian) multipliers, that is about the relative size of the change in money supply or autonomous expenditures necessary to bring about a given change in aggregate demand. As inspection of an $IS/LM$ diagram indicates, the lower is the interest elasticity of the demand for money and the greater the interest sensitivity of expenditures the greater is the efficacy of monetary policy compared to fiscal policy.

Perhaps more importantly, the two schools differ on the relative stability of the Keynesian and money multipliers. The monetarists' belief in a relatively more stable demand for money, a wider and more general effect of monetary policy, and greater stability of expenditures with respect to interest rate changes, establishes the presumption of a more stable money multiplier than Keynesians would expect. Moreover, Friedman's permanent-income theory of consumption suggests a less stable Keynesian multiplier than Keynes's current-income theory, since the effects of changes in autonomous

9 Leijonhufvud, op. cit.
10 In this context, see Stein, J. L., ed., *Monetarism*, Amsterdam, 1976.

expenditures depend on how much of a current change in income is thought to be 'permanent' and this will vary over time, and with particular circumstances.

A third major difference concerns the source of fluctuations in aggregate demand. Keynesians' stress on the instability of corporate investment emphasizes real factors as a major source of changes in aggregate demand. Monetarists, on the other hand, believe that the real economy is more stable, and suggest that monetary factors are a more important source of disturbance.

The differences in 'beliefs' are sustained on both sides by the results of empirical research, and in a sense it is because of the empirical results that the two sides believe what they do. None the less, we have given prominence to the *a priori* differences because these provide the reason why each school prefers one set of results to the other.

These differences of opinion lead to different preferences as to the form of a simplified presentation of the determination of aggregate demand. A simplified monetarist presentation might take the form of the following equation:

$$(1) \qquad\qquad Y = V(r) \cdot M$$

A simplified Keynesian presentation, on the other hand, might look like this:

$$(2) \qquad\qquad Y = m \cdot A(r)$$

where $m$ is the average (rather than marginal) multiplier, and $A$ is the level of autonomous expenditure.

Although these equations may suggest worlds of difference, this appearance is illusory. In fact both *can* be used to represent exactly the same theory with exactly the same presumptions about the empirical magnitudes involved. The reason for this follows from Chapter V: the rate of interest is both a real and a monetary phenomenon since it is determined jointly by the balance between saving and investment and the demand for and supply of money. The $r$ of equation (1) is thus only determined when the $A$ and $m$ of equation (2) are determined, whilst the $r$ of equation (2) is only determined when the $M$ and $V$ of equation (1) are determined. In the same way we could present income and price 'theories' of the demand for goods which embody exactly the same theory and values for the parameters. Belief in the greater size and, more importantly, the greater stability and relevance of the money multiplier of course suggests the adoption of equation (1) rather than equation (2) as a basic paradigm, but the different appearance of the equations should not *itself* be taken to imply a different theory.

The differences on theoretical questions naturally lead on to differences on questions of policy. The monetarists' belief that the money multiplier is larger and more stable than the Keynesian multiplier suggests that monetary policy should be preferred to fiscal policy as a method of influencing aggregate demand. Greater stability also suggests the money supply as a superior indicator and, if it is readily controllable, as a preferable target to the level of interest rates. Monetarists tend to suggest, moreover, that the authorities' control of the cash base can be relied upon for control of the over-all money stock, whereas Keynesians tend to question the workability and desirability of a cash-based system (see Chapter IX) and, having therefore relied on less certain methods of control (if any), are apt to regard the money stock as less readily controllable than the monetarists.

None the less, the monetarist belief that changes in the money supply are the major source of fluctuations in aggregate demand suggests that even monetary policy should be used sparingly as a counter-cyclical device. As we have seen, at the extreme this leads to the advocacy of a fixed monetary rule.

It is both interesting and important to note, however, that the two most radical and far-reaching contentions of the monetarist school, namely the monetary theories of inflation and the balance of payments are challenged by Keynesians not on grounds of monetary theory as such but rather on their assumptions about the real economy. As we saw in Chapter VII, the chief bone of contention in the theory of inflation is not whether the acceleration of inflation has been caused by monetary expansion but whether it has been caused in a fundamental sense by aggregate demand expansion, however the expansion originated. The dispute is, in other words, about the nature of the labour supply function and the ability of institutional developments to influence the trade-off between inflation and unemployment. Similarly, the key differences in the theory of the balance of payments concern the degree of integration of international goods markets and the perfection of domestic substitution relationships.

It is thus perfectly consistent for an economist to take a Keynesian view of the demand for money and yet adopt the position associated with the monetarist, which rejects cost-push as a causal factor. It is true, none the less, that the Keynesian tradition has tended to stress the uniqueness of labour markets and the importance of institutional and sociological factors in the determination of wages.[11]

The implication of a cost-push view of inflation is that an incomes policy (or some major change in the wage bargaining structure) is necessary either on its own, or as a complement to a deflationary monetary policy, to prevent the attempt to stop inflation from resulting in severe unemployment. The implication of a pure demand-pull or monetarist view is that, apart from a possibly beneficial effect on inflationary expectations, such policies are at best unnecessary and ineffective and at worst prejudicial to the efficient working of the market mechanism; a policy of monetary deflation is required in order to reduce both actual and expected inflation before there can be a return to the natural rate of unemployment with stable prices.

[11] See Keynes, *General Theory*, Ch. 21.

# MONETARY DEVELOPMENTS IN THE UNITED KINGDOM

In this chapter we propose to sketch recent monetary developments in the United Kingdom, thus placing the discussion of previous chapters in a particular historical and institutional context.

When the authorities returned to an active monetary policy in 1952 the domestic policy problems were relatively simple: to aid fiscal policy in maintaining full employment without inflation, and to manage operations in the gilt-edged market in which the problems relating to the post-war massive excess liquidity had been eliminated. The concern with growth had not yet arrived on the scene, and inflation, whilst a source of concern, was primarily so because of fears concerning the balance of payments. Indeed for the first two decades monetary policy was almost exclusively associated with recurring balance of payments problems in the context of a fixed exchange rate and a commitment to full employment.

By the early 1960s, however, policy problems were becoming a good deal more complex. Concern over the continuing high levels of growth of output in continental Europe led to the promotion of growth as a key goal of economic policy in the United Kingdom. This lent increased importance to the goals of maintaining a high level of employment, but creeping inflation and consequent deterioration in international competitiveness hindered the attainment of full employment under a fixed exchange rate, and by the mid-sixties the economy was showing signs of a marked change in the trade-off between employment, inflation, and balance of payments goals. In 1967 the authorities tried to resolve this by a devaluation, but they were forced to initiate a substantial deflation in order to make the measure effective. Moreover, the slackness of aggregate demand and a relatively high level of unemployment failed to prevent a wages explosion in 1969, which formed the basis of a marked acceleration in the rate of price inflation in 1970 and an eventual deterioration of the external position. By floating the pound in 1972 the authorities were able to ease the external constraints on domestic expansion and thus make a determined attempt to secure full employment and growth. None the less, conflicts of objectives still prevailed. Fuelled by a sharp deterioration in the terms of trade, but also partly owing to purely domestic causes, inflationary pressure mounted to unacceptable heights, eventually necessitating an abandonment of the employment objective.

If the authorities had accepted monetarist analysis of the causation of inflation, the obvious solution would have been tight control of the money supply to restrict aggregate demand, and acceptance of the temporarily large increase in unemployment which would be necessary to bring down inflationary expectations. Throughout the post-war period they were indeed prepared to use deflation in order to restrain inflation and improve the balance of payments position, but because of the apparent predominance of cost-push forces they were reluctant to rely on this as a sole weapon. Instead they resorted to prices and incomes policies as a way of easing the incompatibilities.

Whatever the effectiveness of such policies, they have been designed and operated as short-term crisis measures and therefore failed to provide the sort of long-term resolution of incompatibilities which the British economy appeared to need. Under these conditions the authorities found themselves unable to achieve their several goals by the deft manipulation and combination of monetary and other policies. Instead they tended to set the policy variables with a view to attaining whichever of their goals seemed most important at the time. Until very recently, the Bank of England did not take much interest in controlling the money stock as such. There were essentially three reasons for this: (i) it placed great importance on the goal of stability of gilt-edged prices (which, as we shall see, conflicts with the goal of money stock control); (ii) since it believed the demand for money was relatively unstable, it regarded interest rates and credit conditions as better indicators; (iii) it believed that expenditure was largely insensitive to monetary policy.

Scepticism about the potency of money stock control reached

a peak with the publication of the Radcliffe Committee's Report. In a now famous passage the Committee pronounced: '. . . we cannot find any reason for supposing, or any experience in monetary history indicating that there is any limit to the velocity of circulation.'[1]

In common with a number of previous surveys,[2] the Radcliffe Committee found that the response of expenditure to changes in interest rates was rather weak, and hence saw a very limited role for monetary policy. Moreover, in so far as the authorities were to try to use monetary policy at all, they should try to act on the liquidity position as a whole rather than on the quantity of money.

What precisely the Radcliffe Report meant by the liquidity position as a whole, and how far it could, however defined, influence the level of aggregate demand subsequently became the subject of much discussion, including some analysis in preceding editions of this book. The report reflected the abnormal post-war situation of massive excess liquidity in which control of the money supply was virtually impossible, and all we need now note is that the authorities apparently accepted Radcliffe's general views on the relative insignificance of the money stock. It was therefore perfectly consistent with its Keynesian views on the transmission mechanism for the Bank to execute monetary policy through operating on interest rates directly rather than through control of the money stock. Although never formalized as such, the Bank of England therefore adopted a sort of general index of interest rates and credit availabilities as both the best indicator and in a loose sense the best target of monetary policy.

During the 1960s the foundations for this view began to be seriously challenged. From the work of Milton Friedman and his associates in the United States there began to emerge a picture of a much more stable demand for money than had previously been supposed. Although the results for the United Kingdom were never as impressive as for the United States, the assumption of gross instability was undermined. Friedman

---

1 *Radcliffe Report*, para. 391.

2 See, for instance, Andrews, P. W. S., 'A further inquiry into the Effects of Rates of Interest'; *Oxford Studies in the Price Mechanism*, ed. Wilson, T., and Andrews, P. W. S., Oxford, 1951, pp. 51–67.

claimed to have shown, moreover, that the interest elasticity of the demand for money was relatively small (thus throwing more of the burden of response to monetary changes on to nominal income) and that the range of expenditures affected by monetary policy was much broader than had been supposed. As the decade progressed, evidence began to accumulate supporting a much stronger and wider impact of interest rate changes on expenditure. This may, to some extent, reflect the fact that there had been a transition from a low-interest regime with small absolute variation to a regime of high rates and large absolute variation.

These theoretical developments, combined with the change from substantial government deficit to substantial surplus in 1969–70 (thus easing pressure on the gilt-edged market), prompted the Bank to move closer to a position of money stock control when in 1971 it adopted a new system of monetary arrangements (to be analysed below), entitled *Competition and Credit Control* (*CCC*).

Events since 1971 have, however, called into question the stability of the demand for money, as previously understood. Although future research may reveal the underlying stability of a redefined money demand function, it is important that the stability of the demand function for M3, accepted by the Bank at the time, appeared to collapse completely. The fact that this happened less to the demand function for M1 may suggest that the authorities should simply treat M1 as the significant monetary aggregate, but as arrangements stood up to 1977, they could not control M1, since their control instrument operated on M3 of which M1 is only a part. This could still leave M1 as a good indicator but not a good target. Although this may be taken to suggest that the authorities should switch to a system devised to control M1 rather than M3, it is not at all clear that, if they did so, the relative stability would endure. After all, within the constraints imposed on M3, M1 has been free to adapt to the needs of trade. It is not unreasonable to believe that this does not provide a firm test of the stability of M1 if put under pressure. If its relative stability were to collapse it would not only fail to provide a useful target, but it would also cease to serve as a reliable indicator.

A further recent development, associated with the terms on

which loans were obtained from the I.M.F., has been the adoption by the United Kingdom authorities of announced ceilings on the rate of growth of the Public Sector Borrowing Requirements (*PSBR*), Domestic Credit Expansion (*DCE*), and the broadly defined money stock, M3.[3] Although originally proposed as ceilings, the specified figures have been widely interpreted as targets, and, given that the authorities are already under pressure from many quarters because the ceilings are taken to be too restrictive, it seems likely that they will have to be operated as targets. The rationale for this change of policy is not altogether clear, but it seems likely that its main justification lies in its possible beneficial effect on inflationary expectations and trade union militancy rather than as a method of preventing the authorities from misusing information and thus destabilizing the economy.[4]

The aggregates M3 and *PSBR* and *DCE* have been defined in Chapter III but some comment is called for at this point on the concept of *DCE* as a target for monetary policy.

It is not known why the authorities adopted *DCE* as a target, but it is clear that the I.M.F. favours it and indeed that a theoretical case can be made for viewing it as a superior target to the money supply, under certain circumstances.[5] If the authorities' goal is some value for the balance of payments then a *DCE* target will always be preferable to a money supply target, whatever the nature of the disturbances to the system. Since (broadly speaking) *DCE* equals the change in the money supply plus the balance of payments deficit, given the maintenance of the target value for *DCE*, any change in the balance of payments, whether originating from the foreign or domestic side, will cause an equal and opposite change in the money supply which (via its effects on interest rates and aggregate demand) will counteract the original disturbance.

If the goal is some value for domestic aggregate demand, however, matters are not so simple. If the disturbance comes

[3] The Chancellor's Letter of Intent to the I.M.F. of 15 December 1976 specified figures for *DCE* and *PSBR*, and these were subsequently reaffirmed in July 1977; see Chancellor of the Exchequer, *The Attack on Inflation after 31st July 1977*, H.M.S.O., London, July 1977, para. 33.

[4] See Chapter VIII.

[5] See Polak, J., and Argy, V., 'Credit Policy and the Balance of Payments', *I.M.F. Staff Papers*, March 1971.

from the domestic side (and provided that expansions of aggregate demand cause deteriorations in the balance of payments, and contractions cause improvements), then $DCE$ is again superior to the money supply, for changes in the balance of payments then lead to changes in the money supply which counteract the disturbance. If the disturbance comes from the balance of payments side, however, then the money supply is superior, for with a fixed value for the money supply the monetary effects of changes in the balance of payments are sterilized, whereas with a fixed value for $DCE$ (and hence a variable money supply) the monetary effects of changes in the balance of payments are transmitted to the domestic economy.

This perhaps provides a theoretical justification for the Governor of the Bank of England's view that focus on $DCE$ as a control variable is appropriate, 'especially when the need remains to rectify our external payments position'.[6]

The authorities' views on the objectives of policy and the place of money in the economic system have played a crucial part in their choice of systems for controlling the money supply, a subject to which we must now turn.

In Chapter II we explained how the authorities could achieve control of the money supply through operating on the cash ratio, yet it is clear that, despite the fact that the banks have been required since 1946 to adhere to a minimum cash ratio specified by the Bank of England, the authorities have not in practice chosen to use this as a fulcrum for control.

In order to understand the reasons for this we must first elaborate with regard to the structure of the United Kingdom money market. In the United Kingdom banks make provision for variations in their cash requirements by holding money market assets consisting of trade bills, Treasury bills, and short-term loans to the Discount Market. The Discount Market uses the funds borrowed from the banks to hold short securities, chiefly Treasury bills. These funds are withdrawable on call by the banks because the Discount Market can call upon the Bank of England to act as lender of last resort.

To understand the functioning of this system let us assume that the Bank calls for Special Deposits from the banks and that they respond by calling in money lent to the Discount Houses.

[6] *Bank of England Quarterly Bulletin*, March 1977, p. 49.

The Discount Houses are now short of cash; in the short run they will replenish this by borrowing from the Bank of England. If the Bank insists on lending at a penal rate, however, the Discount Houses will incur losses on their excess holdings of Treasury Bills. They will then try to sell Treasury Bills, or, what comes to the same thing, take up fewer Bills at the weekly tender. Now since 1939 there has been a convention that the Discount Market should 'cover the tender', that is, take up all Treasury Bills not bought by higher bidders. In order to reduce their holdings of Treasury Bills, the Discount Houses would thus have to lower their bid at the weekly tender.

The effect of the banks calling in money from the Discount Market is thus the same as a reduced holding of trade bills or Treasury Bills by the banks, provided that the Bank of England lends at a penal rate. Once the Discount Houses have unloaded Treasury Bills, a multiple contraction of bank assets and liabilities will ensue; the Bills will be paid for ultimately with money drawn from the banks. This will reduce the banks' cash and deposits by equal amounts and hence make them short of cash. They will again respond by liquidating some of their money market assets and the process will continue until deposits have been reduced by $1/\beta$ times the reduction in cash.

It is of course necessary for the efficiency of this policy that the authorities accept some flexibility in the Treasury Bill rate and other short rates which are closely linked to it. They have been reluctant to do this for a number of reasons. The authorities have tended to believe that financial markets are dominated by operators with extrapolative expectations and short planning periods whose major concern is with expected changes in interest rates rather than with the current levels. A rise in rates might then lead to a decreased rather than increased demand for securities as operators hold off in anticipation of further rises. Given that sharp swings in Treasury Bill rates might spread to the short (and even perhaps the long) end of the gilt-edged market, they might threaten the authorities' objectives with regard to financing the public debt. This follows because the authorities believe that stability of gilt-edged prices constitutes a distinct advantage to their holders. If this advantage were removed, *ceteris paribus*, it would require a lower average price of gilt-edged to persuade the public to hold a given volume of gilt-edged.

A further apparent drawback to cash ratio control was that, as arrangements stood, large swings in interest rates might threaten the profitability of the Discount Houses. Despite their agreement to cover the tender, the Discount Houses could always attempt to divest themselves of Treasury Bills to satisfy an over-all excess demand for cash by the banks by lowering their bid relative to that of outside tenderers. But if this failed, the Discount Houses, as explained in Chapter II, would have to borrow from the Bank of England at a penal rate, thus making losses on their excess holdings of Treasury Bills.

A third possible cause of anxiety lay in the fact that the Treasury Bill rate is a key determinant of short rates generally and that flows of foreign capital are especially sensitive to short rates, a crucial matter given the special position of London as one of the leading international reserve centres. In the light of the above considerations, the authorities chose to make Treasury Bills interchangeable with cash at virtually fixed rates of interest, thereby forfeiting control of the cash base.

For a long time the banks had adhered to a 'prudential' minimum liquid assets ratio of 30 per cent, which was formalized in 1957 and reduced to 28 per cent in 1963; the minimum cash ratio was 8 per cent. In 1959 the Radcliffe Committee enshrined in its report a precise statement of what came to be called the 'new orthodoxy' of monetary control based on a liquid asset ratio. The statement was: 'The supply of Treasury Bills and not the supply of cash has come to be the effective regulatory base of the domestic monetary system.'[7] Even before Radcliffe it had been noted that this proposition 'looked like developing into the popular monetary fallacy of the decade'.[8] Much controversy ensued,[9] but over the next ten years the proposition was utterly refuted by the facts. Since the Bank of England persists in

[7] *Radcliffe Report*, para. 583.

[8] Newlyn, W. T., *The Economist*, 9 December 1957.

[9] For authoritative statements of the new orthodoxy, see: Dacey, W. M., 'The Floating Debt Problem', *Lloyds Bank Review*, April 1956; King, W. T. C., 'Should Liquidity Ratios be Presented?', *The Banker*, April 1956; and Sayers, R. S., 'The Determination of the Volume of Bank Deposits; England 1955–56', *Quarterly Review of the Banca Nazionale del Lavoro*, December 1955. For the contrary view, see: Coppock, D. J., and Gibson, N. J., 'The Volume of Deposits and the Cash and

→

relying on a liquid assets fulcrum incorporating additional constraints, it is worth pursuing this issue further.

In order to show that the Treasury Bill supply was not the regulatory base it must be demonstrated that contraction (expansion) of the Treasury Bill supply is neither a necessary nor sufficient condition for a contraction (expansion) in bank deposits.

To demonstrate this the first step will be to show that a contraction in Treasury Bills will not, by itself, induce contraction. We shall assume the banks' liquid assets are initially at the minimum level.

How can a contraction in Treasury Bills come about? It could, of course, result from a reduction of the Treasury's working balances at the Bank of England, but this would clearly not affect the banks' liquidity ratio, since it would substitute cash for Treasury Bills. The only other alternative, assuming government expenditure and revenue to be given, is an increase in some other form of borrowing. This can only be either from the public or from the banks at the expense of loans to the public. In either case deposits must fall by an amount $x$ equal to the reduction in Treasury Bills. This means that with a cash ratio $\beta$ the banks now have excess cash equal to $\beta x$. But by the normal multiplier process they will re-expand deposits up to the limit of $1/\beta$ times their excess cash; deposits will thus return to their original level, provided that it is possible to obtain liquid assets from non-banks to satisfy the minimum liquidity ratio.

So long as they have surplus cash the banks can increase their holdings of liquid assets by:

(i) increasing their share of the total Treasury Bill issue;
(ii) increasing their holdings of private bills;
(iii) increasing their call loans to the discount market.

The third adjustment requires that, *ceteris paribus*, the discount

Liquid Assets Ratios', *The Manchester School*, September 1963; Newlyn, W. T., 'The Supply of Money and its Control', *Economic Journal*, June 1964; and Crouch, R. L., 'The Inadequacy of New "Orthodox" Methods of Monetary Control', *Economic Journal*, December 1964, and 'Money Supply Theory and the United Kingdom's Monetary Contraction 1954/56', *Oxford Bulletin*, No. 2, 1968.

market should reduce its non-bank borrowing, increase its share of the total Treasury Bill issue, or increase its holdings of private bills and short bonds.

The financial statistics showed that there was ample scope for these alternatives, and this has been confirmed by the facts. Between 1959 and 1964 Treasury Bills declined by £839 m.; during the same period banks' liquid assets increased by £126 m. During this period deposits expanded in proportion to banks' cash.

Those writers who propounded the new orthodox view that deposits will expand and contract as a result of an expansion or contraction of the Treasury Bill issue, other things unchanged, were right only in the situation in which the 'back door' of the Bank is always open, which means that the Bank adjusts the market's books each day by the appropriate decrease or increase in cash to accommodate the Treasury Bill issue. This indirect association between the Treasury Bill supply and the level of deposits is thus a special case of the old orthodoxy in which cash is the regulatory base of the domestic banking system, but it is being adjusted, as a matter of policy, to the short-term borrowing requirements of the Treasury.

A further problem with the liquidity ratio system was that if the authorities were to be successful in restraining bank expansion (or for the sake of simplicity, effecting a contraction), this would entail the banks unloading gilt-edged securities on to the market. In this situation the Bank could still maintain control of short rates by continuing to make Treasury Bills interchangeable with cash; but *only* if it were prepared to countenance a fall in gilt-edged prices sufficient to persuade the public to take up the securities unloaded by the banks would it retain monetary control. The effect of this would be to throw the burden of adjustment on to the gilt-edged market.

It is not surprising that, given the Bank's views about the instability of the market, it resorted to other methods of exercising monetary control, including the use of Special Deposits. Moreover, when the banks responded to a request for Special Deposits by selling gilts, the Bank made it clear that this was not acceptable, thereby effectively moving to a constraint on advances. Thereafter the Bank came to exercise control through a variety of direct controls and the so-called 'moral suasion' rather than through operations on the liquidity ratio as such.

Partly as a quid pro quo for these restrictions, but also partly because of its inherent usefulness, the authorities accepted the banking cartel, under which key deposit and lending rates were tied to the Bank Rate. The usefulness of this arrangement lay in the greater predictability of market behaviour, in particular because of the ability of the Bank to control all the major short rates directly through its control of Bank Rate.

Besides its diminishing effectiveness, due to increasing evasions of the controls, this system had two major drawbacks:

(i) it inhibited competition between banks, and hence both misallocated resources and hindered future development;

(ii) it allowed, and even encouraged, the development and expansion of other financial intermediaries, which progressively weakened the importance of that section of the system (commercial banks) over which the authorities had some control.

The new system of control known as Competition and Credit Control (*CCC*),[10] announced in 1971, was designed to introduce a fresh approach to monetary management. The new system embodied four fundamental changes, which were as follows:

(i) Instead of the old 28 per cent liquidity ratio, the banks were now to maintain a 12 per cent reserve assets ratio, but reserve assets were defined much more narrowly than liquid assets. Commercial bills in excess of 2 per cent of eligible liabilities, till money, and refinanceable export credit were excluded from the reserve asset category, but bonds with less than one year to run to maturity were included. These changes were clearly designed to tighten up the loopholes which had existed under the old system. The banks were also to maintain a daily level of cash balances with the Bank of England equal to $1\frac{1}{2}$ per cent of their eligible liabilities. This

[10] See 'Competition and Credit Control', *Bank of England Quarterly Bulletin*, June 1971.

replaced the old 8 per cent cash ratio which, unlike the new one, had included till money.

(ii) Controls were extended to a wider group of deposit-taking institutions.

(iii) The banking cartel was discontinued.

(iv) The Bank announced that it could no longer be relied upon to support the long end of the gilt-edged market, although it would still support gilts with less than one year to run to maturity, and might even intervene to support long gilts, but solely at its own discretion and initiative.

Given that the chief reason behind the Bank's previous policies was its concern about the gilt-edged market, the key element in this package was (iv). This enabled it to place 'less reliance on particular methods of influencing bank and finance house lending'[11] and also permitted the abandonment of the cartel. With this privilege gone it was now both fair and expedient that control should be extended across the whole banking sector. The only element of the package which did not entirely fit was the Bank's choice of a liquidity ratio rather than cash ratio as the fulcrum for control. This rather suggested that the change of view by the Bank had not been as extensive as was implied.

This was indeed confirmed by subsequent events. Having failed to stem the currently rapid increase of M3 despite large rises in interest rates, in December 1973 the Bank introduced a Supplementary Credit Control Scheme by which banks were obliged to submit funds to the Bank of England, without payment of interest, in relation to the increase of their interest-bearing eligible liabilities (*IBELs*) over and above some specified rate, to be announced periodically by the Bank. Since the proportion to be submitted increased with the size of the excess, it constituted a progressive penalty. This system of control has subsequently become known as 'the corset'.

The purpose of this scheme was clearly to limit the banks' incentive to compete for funds in response to a contractionary move by the Bank. This would then limit the rise in short rates generally and the Treasury Bill rate in particular. The system

11 'Competition and Credit Control', loc. cit., p. 189.

was thus another attempt by the Bank to attain a better trade-off between its objectives of money stock control and debt management.[12] The scheme clearly operated partly counter to the spirit of *CCC* but it did appear to allow more scope for competition than a return to ceilings on lending to the private sector, for although the banks were still subject to qualitative guidance, they were relatively free to choose their preferred allocation of funds between public and private debt, and they could still compete effectively for non-interest-bearing deposits. The scheme was suspended in February 1975, re-introduced in November 1976, and suspended again in August 1977.

The foregoing account of monetary developments in the United Kingdom illustrates a number of important elements in the application of monetary policy, some of which are specific to the particular period. Those which are specific to the United Kingdom are to some extent a reflection of the historical development of the institutions of the City of London and of the firm attachment to the Keynesian tradition of macro-economic thought. The former has built up strong interests in the pre-servation of the particular structure of the money market requiring second best methods of monetary control. The latter has tended to preserve the Keynesian paradigm intact, not-withstanding developments in theory, partly due to monetarist innovation, which delayed synthesis both in the literature and as a basis for policy. This time lag was facilitated by the pre-dominance of fiscal policy in the post-war period in which monetary policy was sterile both because of the massive excess liquidity resulting from war-time constraints on consumption and a prevailing philosophy that cheap money was beneficial to development and in any case minimized the burden of the interest on the disproportionately large post-war national debt.

We have already briefly described the complications facing policy-makers when the combination of inflation and growing unemployment was superimposed on the structural problem of the inability of the economy to export sufficient marketable manufactured goods to match the high marginal propensity to import at full employment growth. Meanwhile the Bank of

[12] For a suggested alternative means of obtaining the same end, see Courakis, A. S., 'Monetary Policy: Old Wisdom Behind a New Facade', *Economica*, February 1973.

England had been reluctantly driven into a situation in which the banks were increasingly unwilling to accept directives which ran counter to their own interests but which had to be increasingly detailed and comprehensive to overcome circumvention. In the second edition of this book, a passage in the policy chapter, drafted in 1970, suggested that the logical conclusion of this process might involve bringing the banking sector into public ownership. As we have seen, the solution of that problem was a dramatic move in the opposite direction with the introduction of $CCC$ in 1971. Unfortunately the authorities had underestimated the impact effect of the banks adopting high-pressure salesmanship, which resulted in an unprecedented increase in $DCE$.

After this initial burst of competition and a pause in incomes policy in favour of a new industrial relations act, the introduction of the new approach to credit control made it reasonable to suppose that analysts would, at last, have an opportunity for identifying and assessing the effects of monetary policy. However, the statutory wage and price freeze in November 1972 initiated another series of 'phases' of incomes policy varying in objectives and effectiveness. We were thus cheated of the opportunity to conclude this chapter appropriately with an analysis of the effectiveness of monetary policy since 1971, and reluctantly we have to end the book 'not with a bang but a whimper'.

## The Appendices

*Appendix* 1

The text of the 'letter of intent' sent by Mr. Healey to the I.M.F. on 14 December 1977 is reproduced as a summary of the situation and prospects at that time, against which readers of this edition will be able to assess subsequent events.

*Appendix* 2

Though this comment on *Radcliffe* is somewhat dated, it remains relevant to the dispute between cash and liquidity control.

# APPENDIX 1

## LETTER OF INTENT

The following is the text of the letter of intent sent by the Chancellor of the Exchequer, Mr. Healey, to the International Monetary Fund on 14 December 1977.

In my letter of 15th December, 1976, I described the programme adopted by the United Kingdom to strengthen the balance of payments over a three-year period, to create the conditions for a reduction in the high rates of inflation then prevailing, and to provide a basis for sustainable growth in output, employment, and living standards. During the first year of our stabilization programme the confidence of the financial markets has returned, the external payments position has strengthened markedly and a decisive turn in the pace of inflation has been achieved.

The maintenance of the social contract with the trade union movement, which kept the growth of average earnings to 8 per cent in the year ending July 1977, has been crucial to this success. The moderation of pay settlements, together with an improvement in our terms of trade and the pursuit of firm financial policies, has led to a marked slowing down in the growth of retail prices.

The year-on-year rate of increase had already fallen from 17·7 per cent in June to 14·1 per cent in mid-October, and since the spring the underlying rate has been well below the annual rate. This justifies the expectation that the annual increase will fall below 10 per cent by the middle of 1978.

The successful application of the system of cash limits and the use of the contingency reserve as a means of keeping expenditure within the published plans have helped to establish firm control over public spending. The ratio of public expenditure to national income has been reduced. Combined with buoyant revenues and a steady improvement of the finances of the public enterprise sector, this has helped to provide room for further tax reliefs, increased social benefits and assistance to the construction industry.

The return of confidence in sterling produced massive inflows of capital which have increased our foreign reserves to over $20 billion by the end of November. These inflows inevitably injected additional liquidity into the economy while exerting persistent upward pressure on the exchange rate. In presenting the 1977–78 Budget I stated the Government's intention of keeping Domestic Credit Expansion (DCE) in 1977–78 well within the limit of £7·7 billion set out in my letter of 15th December, 1976, and of maintaining control of the growth of the money supply.

The growth of sterling M3 in 1977–78 was forecast as being in the range 9–13 per cent. In recent months, the inflow of overseas funds was reaching the stage at which it was putting the control of the money supply at risk. The Government accordingly felt it necessary to change its intervention tactics in the exchange market in order to remove that risk and to maintain the counter-inflationary thrust of its monetary policies.

Following this change short-term interest rates adjusted to a level appropriate to my domestic monetary objectives. The Government remains convinced of the need to provide a stable framework of financial policy on which to build an enduring recovery of the economy in the next year and beyond.

These major improvements in the economic situation during 1977 have not, as yet, been accompanied by a resumption of significant economic growth. The fiscal measures announced in October, 1977, were designed to strengthen the forces of recovery. Provided earnings can be held within the Government's objectives, growth of about $3\frac{1}{2}$ per cent per annum should be attainable between the second half of 1977 and the second half of 1978 and should be consistent with achieving a significant current account surplus in both 1977–78 and 1978–79.

The benefits of North Sea oil will create the conditions in which it should be possible to maintain a surplus on the current account for a number of years. This will be needed to help meet the United Kingdom's external debt repayment obligations and to contribute to the financing of structural capital flows including those arising from export credit.

The scope for stimulating the economy further will depend to an important extent on the competitive performance of British industry and on the movement of costs and prices. The industrial strategy is intended to achieve a marked improvement in the trading performance of British industry at home and overseas. Measures to improve productivity, raise investment and encourage retraining are important and continuing aspects of Government policy, and they have the support of management and unions.

We have however to take account of past increases in domestic costs higher than those of most other industrial countries and of the recent appreciation of sterling. Large improvements in performance cannot be achieved quickly and the burden of protecting the United Kingdom's competitiveness and thus employment will continue to fall squarely on the containment of domestic costs. We have therefore striven, in close consultation with the Trades Union Congress and the Confederation of British Industry, to contain the growth of average earnings within limits which will secure deceleration of inflation to single figures by the middle of next year and thereafter progressively approach the price performance of our competitors in world markets. We shall now be building on the successes so far achieved in countering inflation, and cooperating with our social partners over the next years in order to ensure an increase in employment and a rise in living standards. This is the only way in which we can by our own efforts bring about a significant and sustained reduction in our present unacceptably high level of unemployment.

In its approach to the exchange rate, the Government will follow a flexible policy, with the objectives of avoiding disruptive fluctuations in the rate, maintaining monetary guidelines and preserving the competitive position of British industry. In other policies which affect the exchange rate the Government will take account of these objectives.

The Government is determined to continue its firm control of public spending, and the counter-inflationary thrust of its monetary policies. It will maintain orderly conditions in financial markets. These will require both control over the money supply and moderation in DCE. DCE for the financial year so far has been well below the level which I originally envisaged: this has been associated with the substantial inflows of overseas funds.

This situation has ended with the change of exchange market tactics and I expect DCE to come back nearer to the levels envisaged earlier, and possibly to make up some of the earlier shortfall. Nevertheless, I expect DCE in 1977–78 and the first quarter of 1978–79 together to be within the total of £7·7 billion earlier envisaged for 1977–78 alone. In addition, I expect the Public Sector Borrowing Requirement for 1978–79 not to exceed the figure of £8·6 billion referred to in paragraph 14 of my letter of 15th December, 1976.

I shall take account of these considerations in deciding whether the prospects for the economy, and particularly for wage settlements and prices, make it possible for me to give a stimulus to the economy in my Budget for 1978–79. During next May on the occasion of the normal Article VIII consultation I expect to review policies further with the Fund for the final period of the standby, which expires on January 2nd, 1979, unless the Government decides before that date that continuation of the standby is no longer necessary.

The Government reiterates its intentions expressed in paragraph 24 of my letter of 15th December, 1976 and, in particular, its firm opposition to generalized restrictions on trade, and does not intend to introduce restrictions on imports for balance of payments reasons. The Government has stated that it is prepared, in current economic circumstances, to consider the further use of temporary selective measures where particular industries which are viable in the long term are suffering serious injury as a result of increased imports. It remains the Government's intention to reduce such selective measures as exist as soon as circumstances permit.

The United Kingdom is determined to make its fullest contribution to the expansion of world trade. But its capacity to do so will depend on how fast other countries expand and on their willingness to maintain open markets and non-discriminatory trading arrangements.

# APPENDIX 2

## THE RADCLIFFE REPORT:
## A SOCRATIC SCRUTINY.*

After the style of Professor D. H.
Robertson's Socratic dialogue in
'British Monetary Policy', *Lloyds
Bank Review*, May 1939.

SOCRATES. I understand that there has recently been an authoritative report on the working of your monetary system?

ECONOMIST. That is indeed so Socrates—the Report of the Radcliffe Committee, composed of men of great ability and wisdom.

S. I have taken some interest in the past in the working of your monetary system; I should be most interested to hear what new light this report has thrown on the subject.

E. The report gives a great deal of very valuable factual data, but it also reflects significant changes in the theoretical analysis of domestic monetary policy.

S. Indeed? Then it may be that the ideas which I have obtained from reading your text books require some correction?

E. It may be so Socrates.

S. Pray expound the new doctrine.

E. I think the doctrine might be summarized in four propositions taken from the report, as follows:

  (i) '... the supply of Treasury Bills and not the supply of cash has come to be the effective regulatory base of the domestic banking system' (Para. 583);

 (ii) '... only very limited reliance can be placed on the interest incentive', as an influence on total demand. (Para. 397);

(iii) '... it is the liquidity position as a whole upon which the authorities must act' (Para. 312);

(iv) '... monetary action works upon total demand by altering the liquidity position of financial institutions and of firms and people desiring to spend on real resources; the supply of money itself is not the critical factor'.

* Newlyn, W. T., *Banker's Magazine*, January 1960, reproduced with the permission of the Editor.

S. From what I have learnt previously the second proposition does not surprise me, but I have difficulty in reconciling the other propositions with some of your text books. Kindly expound them.

E. Certainly Socrates. The first proposition is the result of the arrangements which have been made to ensure that the Government can always lay its hands on the funds necessary to discharge its day-to-day obligations.

S. Am I right in believing that this is one of the functions of the Bank of England as the Government's banker?

E. By no means Socrates. It is the view of the Bank of England that such provision would be inflationary because Treasury borrowing from the Bank of England expands the cash base thus allowing a multiple expansion of bank credit.

S. Indeed! This view, if I may say so, appears to be based on the text book account of these matters rather than on the version contained in your propositions.

E. So it would appear.

S. But if the Bank of England does not perform this function who does?

E. You must understand Socrates that it is one of the most important functions of the discount market to supply the Treasury with funds. The discount houses, acting together as a syndicate, are under an obligation to 'cover the tender'—that is to say the syndicate have to take up all bills which cannot be sold to 'outside' lenders at a better price.

S. That is certainly a great convenience for the Government, but have the discount houses always got sufficient funds?

E. No, not always. In such a situation the authorities must act to avoid a disturbance in the market.

S. What do you mean by a disturbance?

E. The excess demand for funds would force up the price.

S. I understand that to be the nature of a market.

E. Yes, but the short term money market has special significance in that it affects foreign confidence in sterling and the authorities regard it as important that there should be a stable short term rate.

S. I see. Now explain to me how the authorities act.

E. In order to maintain a stable short term rate the authorities make cash available in the market if the discount houses haven't enough.

S. By the authorities do you mean the Bank of England?

E. I suppose I do.

S. Then this cash which the Bank of England makes available to the discount market for loan to the Treasury is thought to be in some way less inflationary than if it were lent directly? Does the Committee approve these arrangements?

E. The Committee does not actually condemn them Socrates. The report says that the assumptions on which the need for this artificial short term market is based are open to question (Para. 585) and expresses 'doubts whether a reversal of all this would now have any catastrophic results for the Treasury' (Para. 587).

S. Indeed! I would have thought it pertinent to consider whether the arrangements themselves might not have catastrophic results for the economy. I understand you to say that it is a result of this stable rate arrangement that 'the supply of Treasury Bills and not the supply of cash has come to be the effective regulatory base of the domestic banking system'. Pray how does that follow?

E. The banks are obliged to hold 30 per cent of their assets in liquid form; this means cash or bills or short term loans to the discount market. Since the banks can get cash by calling money from the market, thus forcing the Bank of England to create more cash, the cash ratio is of no significance; it is the liquid assets ratio which restricts bank lending. Hence bank-credit is based on total liquid assets not on cash.

S. But are not rather more than two-thirds of these liquid assets themselves bank credit?

E. They are indeed Socrates.

S. So that if we want to explain what it is that bank credit *as a whole* is based on, we must still say 'cash'?.

E. I suppose we must. But since the authorities wish to have a stable short term market, cash is a passive element.

S. What this seems to me to amount to is that bank credit is still based (just as the older text books say) on cash, but the authorities have chosen to allow the cash base to be determined by requirements other than the requirements of monetary restriction.

E. That is a reasonable interpretation Socrates but there remains the ability of the authorities to control bank credit (I beg your pardon —I mean the *rest* of bank credit) by altering the supply of Treasury Bills.

S. How is that done?

E. Simply this—if the banks are deprived of Treasury Bills of an amount equal to $x$, their obligation regarding liquid assets forces them to contract credit by $\frac{10}{3}x$.

S. But how does the Treasury dispense with the need to issue $x$ Treasury Bills—do you mean that the government cuts its expenditure by that amount?

E. Certainly not Socrates—the budgetary requirements must be taken as a datum. The Treasury dispenses with the bills by *funding*. That is to say the issue of long term securities in their place.

S. Who buys the securities?

E. The public.

S. So that this is not simply 'funding' but a switch from borrowing from the banks to borrowing from the public?

E. That is so. The net effect is to reduce deposits and the banks' Treasury Bill holdings by $x$, as a result of which they will have to contract credit by $\frac{10}{3}x$.

S. Wait—I am a little perplexed. The operation so far has not affected the bank's cash, since the borrowing on bonds is exactly offset by the repayment of bills, but the sale of bonds will reduce deposits by $x$, thus leaving the banks with $x/12$ surplus cash. Rather than contract will the banks not try to get a larger *share* of the outstanding Treasury Bills? Or lend to the discount houses on short bonds? Or even lend to their customers by way of bills? And will this not cause a re-expansion of $x$, leaving the volume of bank credit as it was before the funding? Indeed it would appear to me that the only result would be a fall in the short term rate of interest.

E. There is something in what you say Socrates—I must have left something out.

S. Could it be cash?

E. Ah yes of course: obviously the authorities would need to take the $x/12$ surplus cash out of the market at the same time as contracting Treasury Bills.

S. If I may say so that is not at all obvious from the statements you have quoted from the Committee. It seems that for a contraction of $x$ in bank money it is still a *necessary* condition that cash should be contracted by $x/12$—just as the older text books tell us?

E. That is so, but this cannot happen unless Treasury Bills are contracted in proportion.

S. Can it not? Could not the Treasury get a larger proportion of its bills taken up outside the banking system by accepting a lower price?

E. Certainly not Socrates—that would cause a rise in the short term rate and ——

S. Yes, yes—I remember, you told me about the short term rate. So that contraction of the cash base is not a *sufficient* condition for monetary contraction simply because the authorities choose to adopt a certain interest rate policy rather than because of any change in the nature of the monetary system?

E. That is so.

S. Now tell me about 'the liquidity position as a whole', on which I understand the Committee places great emphasis. How does the Committee define liquidity?

E. Well, the Committee doesn't actually *define* liquidity anywhere, Socrates, but it appears to mean 'the ease or difficulty encountered by spenders in their efforts to raise money for the purpose of spending on goods and services' (Para. 389). Raising money in this context includes both selling assets and borrowing.

S. This is a most comprehensive definition of the monetary influence on demand but it gives no indication of its elements or manifestations, nor do I understand how the authorities 'act' upon it as stated in your third proposition. I can see, for example, that constraints on spending might result in spenders holding financial assets in excess of normal requirements, but the authorities can't take these away from them by *monetary* measures—except by encashing them! I would have thought that the quantity of money together with the strength of the desire to hold on to it *was* a critical factor and that the power of the authorities to influence the situation rested upon their power to control its supply. How else can the authorities act on 'the liquidity position as a whole'?

E. By 'operations on the structure of interest rates which, for institutional reasons, change the liquidity of financial operators'. (Para. 394).

S. Oh dear! I thought it was the other way round.

E. I think that the difficulty stems from the use of the term liquidity by the Committee in two very different ways.

S. Quite so. It has often seemed to me that there is much to be said for the establishment of a permanent 'inquisition' on the use of terms by professional economists. But pray continue.

E. The important point is that it is through changes in the value of financial assets that monetary action affects demand.

S. Indeed? But according to your second proposition the Committee allows very little strength to the 'interest incentive' effect on spending?

E. That is so.

S. That I understand to mean the response by spenders to changes in the *cost* of obtaining funds.

E. That is my understanding too.

S. But is not a change in the value of financial assets simply one form of a change in the cost of obtaining funds? There is no difference, is there, between a fall in the price which can be obtained for a bond you already hold and a fall in the price at which you can sell a new bond of your own?

E. I agree.

S. If the Committee does not believe that spenders respond to changes in the cost of obtaining funds how do such changes affect demand?

E. According to the Committee through their effect on lenders. A rise in interest rates means that financial institutions can only expand their lending by selling securities at a loss.

S. I know that banks substitute advances for securities when circumstances are favourable, and vice versa, but are there any other institutions which normally act in this way?

E. Not *normally*. Perhaps the point should be made more general. Financial institutions operate by borrowing and lending on different terms: it is thus that they affect the liquidity of spenders. A change in interest rates will inhibit operations because of the increased costs to the financial institutions.

S. Pray why can these financial institutions not pass on the increased cost by raising their lending rate?

E. There are institutional reasons why rates cannot be thus adjusted.

S. What are these institutional reasons?

E. There are certain conventions and agreements regarding rates. Thus the bank's lending rate to the discount houses and the bank's advances rate are related to Bank-rate; they do not reflect what the market will bear.

S. I see. So this 'control' only works to the extent that financial institutions maintain conventions which, in the circumstances in which the control is required, would restrict their profits?

E. As to the effect on profits I am unable to speak—the profits of the banks was not a subject into which the Committee thought it should pry.

S. Did the Committee consider that your financial institutions are flexible and adaptable?

E. Yes indeed—there are several statements which reflect this view.

S. In that case, is not the 'control' on which the Committee places so much emphasis rather unreliable?

E. Should this prove to be the case Socrates the Committee suggests the device of raising the minimum liquidity ratio of the banks, and similar restrictions on other lenders.

S. Does the Committee specify what assets would qualify as liquid assets in the case of the banks?

E. No, I'm afraid it doesn't, but the context would seem to imply that it had in mind those assets which are at present included in 'liquid assets'.

S. This would include commercial bills?

E. It would.

S. Would it not be possible for the banks to satisfy a higher liquidity ratio by the simple device of lending by way of bill (directly or indirectly) instead of by advances, as they used to do in the past?

E. Within limits—yes.

S. Is there any reason to suppose the limits are narrow?

E. No, I think not, from what the Committee says about the increase in bill finance during the recent credit squeeze (Para. 165).

S. So that this control, also, depends on the institutions concerned keeping to present conventions in circumstances in which it would not be in their interest to do so because it would divert business into other financial channels?

E. In the Committee's view such a control would need to be accompanied by restrictions on other financial institutions because they all contribute, as does trade credit, to the 'general liquidity position', but the Committee 'shuddered' at the thought of this.

S. Yes, I follow that—in terms with which I am familiar the banking system determines the volume of money and the other financial institutions and trade credit influence its velocity.

E. Those are not terms which commend themselves to the Committee, Socrates. With regard to velocity the Committee states 'we have not made more use of this concept because we cannot find any reason for supposing, or any experience in monetary history indicating, that there is any limit to the velocity of circulation' (Para. 391). Are you feeling ill Socrates?—you have gone quite pale.

S. How in the name of Aristotle can the question as to whether or not velocity has an absolute limit have any bearing whatever on its validity or utility as a concept? Am I to be asked to abandon the concept of velocity in physics for the same reason?

E. I think the Committee may have meant ——

S. As to this historical generalization would your Committee maintain its position to the extent of claiming that you could manage today with the same quantity of money as you had under your first Queen Elizabeth?

E. I doubt it Socrates.

# INDEX OF AUTHORS CITED*

* Covers only footnote references; substantial textual discussion is included in the Subject Index.

# SUBJECT INDEX

# SURVEYS OF EMPIRICAL WORK

1. *Essays in Money and Banking*, Ed. C. R. Whittlesey and J. S. G. Wilson; Chapter 5, 'Regularities and Irregularities in Monetary Economics', J. L. Harris, Oxford, 1968.
2. *Money in Britain* 1959–1969, Ed. D. R. Croome and H. G. Johnson, Chapter II, 'A Summary of Empirical Evidence', A. A. Walters, Oxford, 1970.
3. *The Demand for Money*, D. E. W. Laidler, Pennsylvania, 1969.
4. 'The Demand for Money Revisited', S. M. Goldfeld, *Brookings Papers on Economic Activity*, 1973, 3.
5. *Money, Information and Uncertainty*, C. A. E. Goodhart, London, 1975.